Growing in Circles

Learning the rhythms of discipleship

Paul Harcourt

RIVER

PUBLISHING

River Publishing & Media Ltd
Bradbourne Stables
East Malling
Kent ME19 6DZ
United Kingdom

info@river-publishing.co.uk

Copyright © Paul Harcourt 2016

All rights reserved. No part of this publication may be reproduced, stored in a retrieval system, or transmitted in any form or by any means, electronic, mechanical, photocopying or otherwise, without the prior written consent of the publisher. Short extracts may be used for review purposes.

Scripture quotations are taken from Holy Bible, New International Version®, NIV® Copyright ©1973, 1978, 1984, 2011 by Biblica, Inc.® Used by permission. All rights reserved worldwide.

Published in partnership with New Wine Trust
www.new-wine.org

ISBN 978-1-908393-63-0
Cover design by www.spiffingcovers.com
Printed & bound by MBM Print SCS Ltd, Glasgow

Contents

What Others Are Saying...   04

Thanks   07

Chapter 1 – Growing in Circles   09

Chapter 2 – Being Disciples   21

Chapter 3 – Intimacy leads to affirmation   37

Chapter 4 – Affirmation leads to identity   51

Chapter 5 – Identity leads to authority   63

Chapter 6 – Authority leads to destiny   77

Chapter 7 – Destiny leads to obedience   91

Chapter 8 – Obedience leads to intimacy   105

Chapter 9 – Spiralling upwards   117

About the author   128

What others are saying...

"My friend Paul Harcourt is a true Pastor and a leader's coach for building genuine, Christlike community. *Growing in Circles* is a must read. Having ministered with Paul in conferences and in his church, I know that he writes from authentic and fruitful experience."

Robby Dawkins, conference speaker, bestselling author, pastor and equipper of churches to do what Jesus did.

"Paul is an experienced leader in both the local and national Church and a man of great integrity, wisdom and influence. *Growing in Circles* is an insightful and inspiring read, as well as a great tool for anyone wanting to go deeper in their relationship with God and grow in their maturity as a believer. I highly recommend it!"

Nicola Neal, Founder and Ceo, Revelation Life, author of Journey Into Love.

"We Christians are often big on desiring spiritual growth, but short on knowing what that really looks like. With great insight, Paul helps us to recognise the cyclical nature of spiritual development and then challenges us to find the rhythm of a faith-filled and supernatural life. This is a seriously helpful and challenging book, whether you are a church leader looking to encourage others, or simply a Christian who wants to grapple

with growing as a disciple in a consumer-driven world."
Cathy Madavan, Speaker and author of Digging for Diamonds.

"Most Christians I encounter want to become more like Jesus. However, so many are paralyzed or stuck in that process. In *Growing in Circles*, Paul offers a succinct and clear way forward. This timely, yet brief read, is straightforward and profound, painting a biblical picture of how the rhythms of true discipleship bring about the transformed life. If you are stuck, or ever have been, this is a must read!"
Rob Peabody, Co-founder and CEO, Awaken movement, Fresh expressions director of pioneer development for the next generation.

"This clearly written, insightful book helps to move us from being observers of the Kingdom of God to those who, by understanding our identity, become participators. This is for everyone who wants to know more about who they are and their destiny. Want to know more about your God given authority? Read this book!"
Lin Button, founder of the Healing Prayer School, counsellor and author.

"Having gotten to know Paul, and seeing him lead in various situations over the last few years, I can say that he lives out what he preaches. He is consistent and godly, so it's no wonder he is also brilliant at giving insight into following Jesus. The older I get, and the longer I am in ministry, the more I am impressed with people like Paul, who really are what they say, because this releases a power and encouragement that not only stretches those of us who have the opportunity to hear him, but challenges us in going after Jesus. You will not be disappointed if you take this journey."

Christy Wimber, conference speaker, author and Senior Pastor of Yorba Linda Vineyard Church

"This is a gem of a read! Paul has been a life-long learner and here he outlines his own spiritual journey into his secure identity as a beloved child of his loving heavenly Father, equipped by the Spirit to minister in the love and power of Jesus to everyone in need. Reading it re-ignites my longing for intimacy with God, my desire to become more like Jesus, my commitment to keep on learning, and my understanding of how to keep on maturing. There is more for all of us, and this book could unlock more of that for you."

John Coles, New Wine

Grateful thanks...

...to John Peters, John and Anne Coles, Lin Button and Reg Walton for stoking the fire.

...to the congregations associated with All Saints' Woodford Wells and to New Wine friends near and far.

...but most of all to Becky. I couldn't ask for a better partner in life, love and leadership.

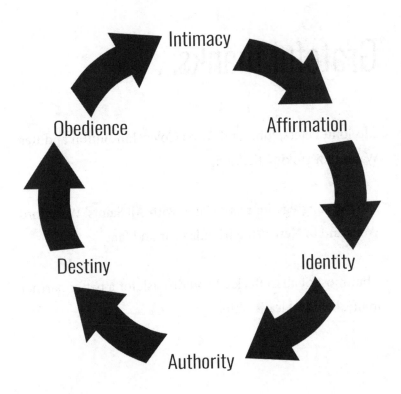

1
Growing in circles

Nature loves circles.

Life on this planet is one of circles and cycles. When biologists look at the processes in nature that make our world habitable, they discover that almost all the essential chemical building blocks of life – carbon, nitrogen, phosphorus, oxygen – go through series of changes, transforming from one state to another, but returning to their starting point repeatedly. Water, another example, evaporates from the earth and condenses into the atmosphere, only to fall again to the earth as precipitation.

Our day is defined as the length of time it takes the earth to rotate once on its axis. Our year is the time it takes for the earth itself to rotate once around the sun. Each of these in turn comes with various phases – the sun rises and sets, but also gives us dawn and dusk each day; seasons come and go as the year develops, each gradually shading into the next.

Things tend not to happen instantly or abruptly. Rather they progress gradually from one thing to the next. Life doesn't stand still.

Clearly this is something deeply embedded in creation, so it perhaps ought not to surprise us that growth in our spiritual life is similar.

Jesus' promise is that his Spirit will enable us to grow into the fullness of life. What I've discovered is that, as with all living and growing things, there are circles and cycles involved. There isn't one key to spiritual growth or one set of practices that we should all adopt; that would be all too impersonal. After all, God is a person who invites us into a relationship where he deals with us each individually. Like any relationship, this develops over time as we give and receive, and as we learn new things about him and about ourselves.

The early Church struggled with teachers who said that there was a "secret, hidden knowledge" that you needed to know in order to progress spiritually. The modern Church struggles with the idea that everything should come quickly and easily. In an age of instant gratification, we look for a quick fix. There is none. There is no secret key to growing spiritually. Growth, in my experience, comes from understanding a few basic spiritual truths more and more profoundly. We will come back to the same places over and over again, but each time experiencing them more deeply. We're not "going in circles" aimlessly, but rather "growing in circles" – learning and growing more like Jesus as we live out the rhythms of discipleship.

From intimately encountering God's love to receiving his affirmation;

From knowing that affirmation to understanding our true identity as his sons and daughters;

From an understanding of our identity to having authority in ministry;

From a grasp of our spiritual authority into the destiny that God has for us;

From a sense of destiny into a life of obedience and purpose that truly satisfies us;

From an obedient walk with God into an ever-increasing awareness of his intimate love;

From that intimacy into a renewed sense of his affirmation, and so on...

This book is about spiritual growth into the image, likeness and imitation of Jesus. This growth is not automatic, and it's not linear. Once you enter into a relationship with God, his Spirit starts to transform you from the inside ... but our experience of the Christian life isn't one where we grow steadily and consistently over time. We seem to go through seasons. Our growth will be by fits and starts. Often we'll feel stuck in our spiritual lives; sometimes there will be something like a "growth spurt". Obviously we're not passive in that development – God calls us to cooperate with his

Spirit. But, even when we do, growth isn't straightforward.

Although spiritual growth doesn't tend to happen steadily, thankfully there are, for all of us, moments or seasons of breakthrough. Often these come because of some change in the environment or an external stimulus. That may be why, for many people, the significant changes in their relationship with God came in their teenage years or early twenties – when everything is changing.

I had the great blessing of growing up in a church-going family. My parents both had church backgrounds, but they've told me that they started attending church regularly again after I was born. I'd like to say that they were overwhelmed by a sense of blessing, but it might equally be that they felt in need of some help!

The church in Harlow in which I grew up was a traditional Church of England church. The worship style varied over the years, depending on the vicar in charge, but was always of a "High Church" tradition. It was the sort of church where the closer you got to the east end the holier things became and the more you would be required to dress up. About the only way of involving young people in the services was to recruit them as servers, so from an early age I grew up carrying things in church and graduated from carrying candles to carrying a cross and finally carrying a book.

I took my involvement in church seriously, but to be honest, no one ever really spent much time explaining the content or meaning of the things that were done in church.

Just as a small example of this, for many years I would come into the church, sit in a pew, kneel down and count to ten. I realise now that people were probably praying and preparing themselves for the service. Not having been taught how to pray, though, it was simply easier to copy the outward form and fit in with what everybody else appeared to be doing rather than ask questions! Nevertheless, something was going on spiritually in my life. I remember having some sort of spiritual experience when I was on a confirmation retreat at the age of 10. As I sat there in Coventry Cathedral, seeing the sun dawn through the immense West End windows, I remember being aware of God in a new way and, as far as I understood the promises that I was making a week later, meant every word I said and took my confirmation very seriously.

Over the next few years in church there would be moments when I felt something of the presence of God. I remember a particular young curate whose preaching was more impassioned than we had been used to from his predecessors. On several occasions I can remember feeling acutely uncomfortable because I thought he was singling me out as he preached – despite there being over a hundred people present. I suspect now that it was God, rather than him, putting me on the spot and speaking directly to me.

Another significant moment was when a tragedy occurred amongst the group of friends that I knew from school. One of our number disappeared and wasn't found for several days. It turned out that he had gone out jogging and been knocked over and killed by a hit and run driver. Naturally, everybody was devastated by this and had all sorts of questions. During that season I found that my faith had resources and a framework to cope with what was happening. It was one of the first times I can remember having to relate my faith to my ordinary, everyday, midweek life, rather than to what happened in church on a Sunday. I will always be incredibly grateful to my parents for making sure that I grew up in church.

Looking back, what I gained from being involved in that church was a sense of God being holy and worthy of our worship. I realise now that I understood God as "the God who made the heavens and the earth", who dwells far from us in unapproachable light. If challenged, I would always have said that I was a Christian, however it didn't really make much difference to my day to day living. Everything revolved around formal services and being in the church building.

When I was 18 I went to university. Up to that point I had never really met anybody from a different church tradition, so I certainly hadn't met any evangelicals. Being from a traditional background, the obvious thing was to be involved with the college chapel, but during the first week there were also lots of "Freshers' Fair" type events. I discovered for the first time that Christians had a Union. I didn't really know what that meant, but I thought, for reasons of solidarity, I should probably be involved! What sealed the deal for me was that the Christian Union were offering free food and so I quickly signed up to be involved in Bible studies.

Despite the fact that I had never read it, I had taken my Confirmation Bible to University with me. You have to understand that, growing up in church, the Bible was read every Sunday, so I was fairly familiar with quite a lot of the stories, but I had never read the Bible for myself personally. I know that for a fact because, when I started to attend the Bible study meetings of the Christian Union, I had to peel the pages apart because of the gold leaf edging! It was a bit embarrassing in lots of ways. The Bible I was using was a different translation from everyone else; I had to look up the location of every book in the index in order to find it and, on top of all that, when I did know where I was going, you would hear me audibly peeling the pages apart to get to the right chapter!

However, reading the Bible had a massive impact on me. In just a couple of months of being away from home in a different environment, my faith exploded. I suddenly realised that God wasn't just the God who made the heavens and the earth and dwelt above us, he had also come alongside us as a friend and a brother. He had appeared to us in a way that we might understand, so that we could get to know him and have a relationship with him. Jesus died on the cross to bear my sin and make that relationship with God possible. By the time I went back home at the end of that first term, I was on fire. I had finally understood for myself who Jesus was, what he had done for me and the difference that it makes to each day.

I really wanted to share this discovery with other people and I soon ended up as one of the leaders of the university Christian Union's "International Student Outreach Team". Basically, we were a group of students who ran a weekly tea party for language school students and overseas academics in Cambridge. People were invited to come together to meet English students and to practice their English. It was quite an attractive offer for the foreign students because, at the end of the evenings, we would often take our guests back with us to formal meals in the dining halls of our colleges.

I'm not quite sure what my college thought of me bringing in ten Japanese girls as my guests, but they never said anything! As well as developing friendship though, the main purpose of the evening was to give our foreign guests an opportunity to study the Bible. Half way through the tea-party portion of the meeting, one of us would stand up and explain that all the team were Christians and invite those who were there, if they wanted, to come with us to another room and to practice their English through a simple Bible study and learn more about what motivated us. That was, for me, one of the most obvious and easiest places to share my faith. Frustratingly, though, it was hard going. In that first year of being involved, I don't remember seeing anybody really come alive in their faith in the way that I had.

That had been playing on my mind and I had been

praying to God that I might see more. I simply wanted more for myself in any case. I realise now that this is a prayer God will always answer for those who pray it persistently.

What happened for me was that, over the course of a week, I began to experience God in a fresh way. I often find it difficult to go to sleep at the end of the day and so developed the practice of having my main time with God as I went to bed. There was a particular week during my second year as a student when, as I was praying and waiting to go to sleep, I would become aware of God in a powerful way. I was filled with a sense of peace and joy. This happened five or six nights in a row. I didn't really know what it meant and I didn't particularly tell anybody about the experience; I assumed that everybody else had been having this experience all along and I was only now catching up.

What I think was happening was that I was experiencing the presence of God in quite a healing way. I had always been a very logical and, in many ways, unemotional person. (I was a mathematician after all). What I found was that the truths I believed in my head were slipping down into my heart. In other words, I discovered afterwards that I was beginning to experience more of what I believed and knew it in a deeper way.

Looking back, however, something else changed. I carried on trying to share my faith with people and I was doing it just as badly as I had done before. However, the results began to be different. We began to see people come to faith through the Bible studies and through conversations with other student friends in the university. Over that next year there was a significant move of God and we saw many people from other parts of the world, including parts that were normally closed to the Gospel, such as Middle Eastern countries or China, come to have genuine encounters with God and become Christians. I knew I wasn't doing anything different, but I came to the conclusion that God was able to work through me in a way that was now more effective.

What I realise now, is that I was discovering that God is not only the God who made the heavens and the earth and who dwells above us in holiness; he is not only the God who comes alongside us as a friend and a brother with whom we can have a relationship; but he is also the God who transforms us from within. Our God is a consuming fire and a powerful presence at work, equipping us to be used in his service. Of course, what I'm describing is experiencing God as Father, Son and then Holy Spirit. God had always been at work in my life as Father, Son and Holy Spirit. What had been inadequate was my understanding.

My spiritual life has continued to grow and develop since then. We're each on our own spiritual journey and we'll probably encounter God in different ways. What I think is fairly consistent is that spiritual growth comes when we experience a fresh revelation of an aspect of God's character, or of ourselves in relationship with him. Many times that will be the result of an experience, an external stimulus that challenges us and causes us to see things differently; through it we discover something new about God and ourselves.

I never intended to write a book! About fifteen years ago David Pytches, the founder of New Wine, prophesied over me that I had a "gift of writing". Fairly soon after that I received a number of invitations to write Bible study notes for various publications, which I have continued to do over the years. Frequently people have asked me whether I was ever going to sit down and write a book. My answer was always that I didn't know what I would write about. I have always felt that I was more of a "generalist" than a "specialist". It didn't appear to me that there was one subject about which I had anything unique to say, or for which I was particularly passionate.

What you hold in your hands now, therefore, is quite a surprise to me. In the last couple of years I have found myself regularly teaching on the relationship between spiritual growth and understanding our identity and authority in Christ. Much of that teaching was in our church, All Saints' Woodford Wells, but I have also shared it with other churches in the UK, and at various New Wine conferences in Sweden, Holland, Finland and the Channel Islands. What I realised as I thought about those various subjects was how closely they fit together, and gradually I came to understand that our spiritual growth as Christians is a never-ending circle of revelation and renewal.

This is a book for people who want to grow. There are many books that give us a vision of living supernaturally, of being involved in signs and wonders, or that inspire us to change the world. Not many, in my experience, give us much help when it comes to how we get from "here" to "there". You may come away from such a book frustrated, not knowing how to start, or feeling that the grip of "how things have always been" is too great to sustain any long-term paradigm shift. I can relate to that. I was captured by a vision of what it could be to follow Jesus, but I didn't arrive at the destination overnight. In fact, I still haven't arrived, but I know that I'm growing towards it with renewed passion.

But what does "spiritual growth" mean? What shape of life are we to grow into? Before we look at the circle of growth and development, let's consider Jesus' agenda for our lives. After all, if we acknowledge that *"God is the potter and we are the clay"* (Jeremiah 18:1-6) what matters is not what we plan for our own lives, but what he desires to make of us. And the great thing is that his plan will be more exciting and more fulfilling than anything you or I could imagine.

2
Being disciples

Through the experience of leading the International Student Outreach Team, I quickly found that I had a passion to be involved in ministry. I also found myself involved in several different expressions of church. The college chapel was very liberal, my home church had been traditional and High Church, and my Christian Union and university church experience was evangelical. With such varied experiences and understandings it's not surprising that I was spending a lot of time reflecting on what church should be like. This process culminated in a very clear call to ministry.

As I had been talking it over with the Lord, there was that sense that he was saying to me, *"So what are you going to do about it?"* I have noticed since in Scripture that God seems to call people in two broad ways, not unrelated but different in emphasis. There are those like Jeremiah who are set apart sovereignly, where the call comes as a clear command; and then there are those like Isaiah who are shown something, who are captured by a vision, and find themselves responding, *"Here am I, send me"* (Isaiah 6:8). For me it was very much the latter experience. I know exactly where I was when I made that response. I was walking back to my room from one of the Christian Union's prayer and praise meetings. I remember praying, "God, I'll do anything you want ... except be a vicar." It's such an oddly specific thing to say, it probably reveals that I had a sneaking suspicion already that that was what the Lord had in store for me.

I went through the Church's selection process for ordained ministry whilst I was still an under-graduate and then, having already committed to work for the local churches developing the overseas students' outreach for a year, went to Wycliffe Hall in Oxford, aged 21. Whilst I knew I was in the right place, I didn't find it easy to fit in. I was one of the youngest in the college and didn't share the same background or experience that many of the other ordinands had. Having only been in evangelical circles for a few years, and without an evangelical home church, it seemed as if everyone else knew each other already and I didn't find it easy to locate points of contact with my fellow students.

Quickly, though, I found my own niche in the life of the college through being part of the football team. Turning out to play once a week was genuinely one of the highlights of that season of my life – although, because I had forgotten to take my shin pads to college, I was constantly getting injured. I had played quite a lot of football so I knew fairly well how long it would take to get over those sorts of bruises and sprains. Some of the other students, however, believed and practiced prayer for healing and kept offering to pray for me. My injuries were always trivial, but nevertheless there was real experience of healing. Every week I experienced an undeniable intervention of God and never missed a game. Whilst it raised issues for me as to why God would bother with things so insignificant – while many people more deserving seemed not receive the answers that they longed for – it did definitely help me realise that God wants to be intimately involved in our lives. As Bill Johnson says, "If it matters to you, it matters to him"[1] – because he is a good Father.

The most significant thing to come out of those experiences of healing, trivial though they were, was an awareness of how God intends us to walk in an intimate relationship of power and partnership. As described in the previous chapter, I had already had experience of the presence and power of the Holy Spirit in my life, but had never met any charismatic Christians who could give me a model for ministry. Simply put, I had been given something but I didn't really know how to give it away to others. One of the fellow students, my friend John Peters, realised that this was the case and took me under his wing. Experientially, I was a charismatic, and I was starting to read the Bible in that way theologically as well, but I was totally lacking in any model which I could follow. Accompanying John on many ministry trips and to lots of meetings, I started to gain a charismatic practice and philosophy of ministry.

Understanding what it is to be a disciple has been one of the most profound revelations I have ever experienced. It has shaped me and my life since as powerfully as any of the experiences described in the first chapter. It seems to me so clear in Scripture and yet I missed it for many years.

When I ask Christians the simple question, "What is the gospel?", I usually find that there are as many answers given as there are people present. Since we all experience the gospel (which simply means "good news") as good news for us personally, perhaps that's not surprising. Some will talk of the love of God, some more specifically about Jesus' saving death on the cross. Some will speak in terms of going to heaven, or having eternal life, or of finding love, meaning or purpose. All these things are true ... but they're not precisely the way that Jesus himself described the content of the gospel.

In Mark 1:14-15 we read, *"After John was put in prison, Jesus went into Galilee, proclaiming the good news of God"* (our English word "gospel" is simply a translation of this phrase, "good news"). *"The time has come,"* he said. *"The kingdom of God is near. Repent and believe the good news (the gospel)!"* The first thing we need to note is that the gospel is not a new message but a new moment. Jesus said,

"*The time has come*", so his good news is that all of the hopes and longings of God's people are now being fulfilled.

Specifically, that means that what the prophets of the Old Testament pointed to has now begun. "The kingdom of God has come near". In other words, the gospel is the coming of the kingdom. What we are called to do is to repent (which means literally to change our minds, to see things in a new way) and to believe (which means to act in accordance with this truth).

An alternative translation for verse 15 can help bring this alive. You could translate this as, "The kingdom of heaven is close at hand." By saying that, Jesus doesn't mean that the time is close because he has already said that, "The time is here." Neither does he mean that the kingdom of heaven is not far away in terms of distance. What he means is that the kingdom is "at hand" – it is present, but we need to take hold of it. I often say to people, "Put out your hand in front of you. That's how close the kingdom of God is." All you need to do is to take hold of it – it's a present possibility, but it demands a response.

Once we understand this, we can see that Jesus' teaching throughout the gospels is focussed on the good news of the kingdom. Jesus' stories, which we call parables, often begin in a similar manner: *"The kingdom of God is like this..."* In other words, the parables describe the nature of this kingdom that the gospel announces. When Jesus' disciples asked him to teach them to pray, this was the prayer that he gave them: *"Our Father in heaven, hallowed be your name, your kingdom come and your will be done on earth as it is in heaven..."* The primary focus of The Lord's Prayer, which is a pattern for our entire prayer life, is the coming of God's kingdom. And what it means for God's kingdom to come is for his will to be done on earth *"as it is in heaven"*.

In other words, we are to pray that things on earth will be as the Father wants them, which is as they are in heaven. There is no sickness or suffering in heaven, no poverty or loneliness, no immorality or injustice. So The Lord's Prayer is that this would be true in our lives and in our communities. It's a prayer for the conditions of heaven to be the conditions of our lives, of the places where we live and of the people with whom we live. Jesus' death on the cross was necessary to break the power of the evil one and to remove the barrier of sin so that we can be restored to God. The purpose of that restoration isn't simply that we all go to heaven when we die, but also that we might be part of the new creation now. And, furthermore, partners with God in bringing it into being.

After the resurrection we read in Acts 1:3, *"After his suffering, he presented himself to them and gave many convincing proofs that he was alive. He appeared to them over a period of forty days and spoke about the kingdom of God."* If you were one of the disciples, imagine all the questions you would have when you discovered that Jesus was risen from the dead! There are so many things that Jesus could have spoken to them about, but his focus tells us so much about what is truly on God's heart. He spoke to them about the kingdom of God.

Acts 1:8 goes on to describe how he tells them to wait for the baptism of the Holy Spirit and how when the Spirit comes, *"You will receive power when the Holy Spirit comes on you and you will be my witnesses in Jerusalem and in all Judea and Samaria and to the ends of the earth."* Nothing is more important to Jesus at that moment than that the disciples understand their part in bringing the kingdom. Kingdom ministry and discipleship are inseparable.

Few Christians who read the Bible have difficulty believing that Jesus performed miracles. Signs and wonders and supernatural evidences of God's goodness are written throughout the gospels, yet most see this as something to do with Jesus and nothing to do with us. Reading the gospel with fresh eyes ought to make us think again. Only he could offer the perfect sacrifice to give us new life; but that life is to be the one that he modelled.

From the beginning Jesus involved his disciples in the miraculous. The implications of that are very significant for our understanding of Jesus theologically and for our own ministries practically. We cannot simply say that Jesus performed miracles because he was God. Philippians chapter 2 tells us that Jesus became a man without ceasing to be God, but that he "emptied himself" of some of the divine powers. Jesus was not omniscient, omnipotent or omnipresent as a man. In other words, he didn't know everything and had to ask questions (*"Who touched me?"*); he didn't have unlimited power (he grew tired and hungry); and he was limited by his human body to being in one place at one time. He did no miracles before his baptism when the Holy Spirit came down from heaven as a dove.

The conclusion is this: Jesus did not do miracles out of his divine nature, as the perfect God, but as a man. That explains how he could pass the ministry of signs and wonders on to the disciples; both his first followers and us today. From the beginning Jesus sought to involve his disciples in doing the things that he did. He didn't simply perform miracles, but demonstrated and modelled what the disciples could do themselves. The first couple of chapters of Mark's gospel are full of stories of healing and deliverance before we come, in chapter three, to the point where Jesus calls the twelve. It says that, *"Jesus went up on a mountainside and called to him those he wanted and they came to him. He appointed twelve that they might be with him and that he might send them out to preach and have authority to drive our demons."* (Mark 3:13-15)

The pattern that Jesus sets is that discipleship involves two dynamics: one is "being with him" (this is drawing close to him, abiding in him and learning from him); the other is "going for him". His purpose in calling these first disciples was *"that he might send them out"* to do the same things that he was doing – *"to preach and to have authority to drive out demons"*. We read later in chapter 6 that this is exactly what they did: *"They went out and preached that people should repent. They drove out many demons and anointed many sick people with oil and healed them"* (6:12-13).

The same emphasis is clear in the record of Jesus' ministry in Matthew and Luke as well. Matthew's gospel has a number of summary statements which describe Jesus' ministry. The first is in chapter 4:23-25:

"Jesus went throughout Galilee, teaching in their synagogues, proclaiming the good news of the kingdom and healing every disease and sickness among the people. News about him spread all over Syria, and people brought to him all who were ill with various diseases, those suffering severe pain, the demon-possessed, those having seizures, and the paralysed, and he healed them. Large crowds from Galilee, the Decapolis, Jerusalem, Judea and the region across the Jordan followed him."

This is what Jesus was doing, day in and day out, during the three years of his earthly ministry.

The summary is repeated again in Matthew 9:35-38, however this time Jesus makes it clear that he is intentionally passing on this ministry to disciples as well.

"Jesus went through all the towns and villages teaching in their synagogues, proclaiming the good news of the kingdom and healing every disease and sickness. When he saw the crowds he had compassion on them because they were harassed and helpless, like sheep without a shepherd. Then he said to his disciples, 'The harvest is plentiful, but the workers

are few."' (verses 35-37)

I have always been encouraged that when Jesus saw the need that was there, he referred to it as a "harvest". Often we can be overwhelmed by the brokenness that we see in the world around us, but Jesus saw it as a harvest, an opportunity for God to reveal his goodness and for people to discover something of his grace and love. However, Jesus also recognises that the workers are few. As he is limited by the incarnation to one human body being in one place at one time, Jesus says that one worker is not enough. His solution is to pray for a multiplication of workers: *"Ask the Lord of the harvest, therefore, to send out workers into his harvest field"* (verse 38). I'm sure the disciples would have heartily agreed with that prayer. What better thing could there be than for there to be more people like Jesus, doing the things that Jesus was doing? They might have been a little less sure when he immediately made them the answer to that prayer!

"Jesus called his twelve disciples to him and gave them authority to drive out impure spirits and to heal every disease and sickness ... 'As you go, proclaim this message: "The kingdom of heaven has come near." Heal the sick, raise the dead, cleanse those who have leprosy, drive out demons. Freely you have received, freely give."' (Matthew 10:1, 7-8). His answer to the great need that he sees in the crowd is for the disciples themselves to go and to preach the same message that he has been preaching and do the same works

that he has been doing. They have received from God, and now is the time to give it away to others.

The same is true of a later occasion reported in Luke 10, this time when Jesus sent 72 disciples. Again, Jesus says,

"The harvest is plentiful but the workers are few. Ask the Lord of the harvest, therefore, to send out workers into his harvest field. Go! I am sending you out like lambs among wolves ... Heal the sick who are there and tell them, 'The kingdom of God has come near to you.'" (Luke 10:2-3, 9)

Jesus trained all of his disciples to preach the same message and to perform the same works. A disciple is not primarily a follower or a student. A disciple is an apprentice. Apprenticeship means that you learn what the master can teach you until you can do those things yourself. That was actually what the whole "Rabbi/disciple" relationship was all about. The way to become a Rabbi was to be a Rabbi's disciple. Disciples would follow their Rabbi closely, observing them in every aspect of life and learning all they had to teach. After a while the disciple would become a Rabbi themselves.

Remember, Jesus could do this because when he performed miracles, he did them not from his divine nature but as a man. That was what it meant to be a disciple of Jesus, and that is what it still means today. At the end of Matthew's gospel we are told that Jesus appeared to them and gave them this commission:

"All authority in heaven and on earth has been given to me. Therefore go and make disciples of all nations, baptising

them in the name of the Father and of the Son and of the Holy Spirit, and teaching them to obey everything I have commanded you." (Matthew 28:18-20)

In other words, as Jesus has trained the disciples, they are to train others who will train others and so on, down to the present day. Though we might feel inadequate, we are no different from Jesus' first disciples and we take comfort in the same promise: *"Surely, I am with you always, to the very end of the age"* (verse 20).

Jesus not only performed signs and wonders as a demonstration of the Kingdom, but also modelled them so that the disciples would be equipped to do them as well. As he said to them in John 14, *"Very truly I tell you, anyone who believes in me will do the works I have been doing, and they will do even greater things than these, because I am going back to the Father. And I will do whatever you ask in my name, so that the Father may be glorified in the Son. You may ask me for anything in my name, and I will do it"* (John 14:12-14).

Whilst many interpreters have assumed that "greater works" must mean "greater in number", the word used for "greater" usually means "greater in degree", i.e. even more dramatic or powerful works, if that were possible to believe! Whatever the correct interpretation, Jesus clearly intends that all of his disciples ("anyone who believes") will understand that they are equipped and called to share in his supernatural ministry of healing and deliverance.

You can see this being put into practice by the disciples

in the book of Acts. The provisional anointing of power and authority that Jesus had given them when he sent them on mission trips was supplanted by the permanent anointing of power and authority that came with the gift of the Spirit at Pentecost. The manuscripts label this book "The Acts of the Apostles". Of course, the book could equally be entitled "The Acts of the Holy Spirit", or especially "The Acts that Jesus continued to do after his Resurrection" (which is what Luke implies in Acts 1:1). However, the title "The Acts of the Apostles" seems to me to helpfully remind us that these are the things that the disciples themselves did, with the power and authority that Jesus had given to them. The disciples did what Jesus had done.

Just by looking at two brief passages in Acts 9 you will see a perfect example of this.

Acts 9:32-35 is the record of Peter's visit to Lydda, where he encountered a paralysed, bed-ridden man called Aeneas. It's instructive to note how Peter is moved to pray: *"Aeneas', Peter said to him, 'Jesus Christ heals you. Get up and roll up your mat'. Immediately Aeneas got up"* (verse 34). Much about this incident is strongly reminiscent of the time, recounted in Mark 2, when Jesus came to "his own town" and friends of a paralysed man lowered him through the roof. Jesus forgave and healed the man with the words *"I tell you, get up, take your mat and go home"* (Mark 2:11). It seems that Peter was doing exactly what he remembered Jesus doing.

Again, in the very next verses of Acts 9, we read of Peter being called urgently to the neighbouring town of Joppa. On this occasion, a much-loved member of the church, Tabitha, had died. Luke notes that she was also known by her Greek name of Dorcas, but the name "Tabitha" is important for this story. When Peter arrived, *all the widows stood around him, crying"* (Acts 9:39). Read carefully what Peter did next:

"Peter sent them all out of the room; then he got down on his knees and prayed. Turning towards the dead woman, he said, 'Tabitha, get up.' She opened her eyes, and seeing Peter she sat up. He took her by the hand and helped her to her feet. Then he called for the believers, especially the widows, and presented her to them alive." (verses 40-41)

If you put that passage alongside Mark 5:21-43, it's hard to escape the conclusion that Peter had in mind what Jesus did when he raised Jairus' daughter:

"When he got to the home of the synagogue leader (Jairus), Jesus saw a commotion, with people crying and wailing loudly... After he had put them all out, he took the child's father and mother and the disciples who were with him, and went in where the child was. He took her by the hand and said to her 'Talitha koum' (which means 'Little girl, I say to you, get up!'). Immediately the girl stood up and began to walk around." (Mark 5:39-42)

I believe that Dorcas' Aramaic name, "Tabitha", reminded Peter of Jesus' spoken command, *"Talitha koum"*, in a similar situation. "Talitha, get up" brought to Peter's mind,

"Tabitha, get up." What his Master and Teacher had done earlier gave Peter not only the faith but also the model for what he, Peter, then did later. The disciples, throughout the Book of Acts, did what Jesus had done.

There is no suggestion in the Bible that these signs and wonders were reserved for the twelve apostles, or for the 72, or for any limited group of people. Neither is there any expectation that the miracles would cease after a period of time. Moving in supernatural power has always been for all believers and for all generations. Even if much of the Church lost this awareness over time, God has never stopped working through ordinary people – miracles have continued in every age. The past century or so has seen a recovery of this truth as something for the whole Church. From the Pentecostal revival have sprung many streams of renewal, including our own New Wine movement amongst others, witnessing to God's desire to make disciples who do what Jesus did.

For me then, "spiritual growth" has taken on a very specific meaning – "becoming more like Jesus". We aren't clones, because God has given us each a unique personality, but his plan for us all is that we might be *conformed to the image and likeness of his Son*" (Romans 8:29). When I say, "becoming like Jesus" (or "being Christ-like"), again I don't believe that we're at liberty to make up our own interpretation of what that means; neither can we pick and choose which part of Jesus' lifestyle and character we want to emulate.

Many people immediately think in terms of "morality" when they hear the word "Christ-like" – things such as Jesus' loving, patient, holy nature, and his faith in God – but if we truly had the character of Jesus, wouldn't it drive us to also do the things that he did? In other words, why not think also in terms of "ministry" when we think of growing in Christlikeness? Additionally, how could we say that we are becoming more like Jesus but have no concern for the last, the least and the lost? Surely "being like Jesus" should also include "ministry" and "mission" then, not just "morality". Spiritual growth includes all of these aspects, and involves becoming more like Jesus in every way.

It is truly the adventure of a lifetime.

Notes

1. Bill Johnson, *Dreaming With God* (Destiny Image, 2006), p7.

3
Intimacy leads to affirmation

If I were to visit an art gallery and look at the paintings of the great masters, I might just stand there and gaze in admiration. Possibly I might feel so moved by what I saw that I would be inspired to take up art. But what I'd seen in the art gallery would be so far beyond the ability of a beginner, would I even know how to start?

William Temple, Archbishop of Canterbury in the 1940s, used to illustrate this point by comparison to Shakespeare:

"It is no good giving me a play like Hamlet or King Lear and telling me to write a play like that. Shakespeare could do it – I can't. And it is no good showing me a life like the life of Jesus and telling me to live a life like that. Jesus could do it – I can't. But if the genius of Shakespeare could come and live in me, then I could write plays like this. And if the Spirit could come into me, then I could live a life like his."[1]

I don't know whether you are a fan of medical dramas such as *Casualty*, *Gray's Anatomy* or *House*, but even if you don't particularly like any of those shows, we all know that a flat line is bad news. Urgent intervention is required! Often that comes in the form of a shock to the system, a "jump start" of electricity, for example, that kicks the heart back into rhythm, pumping blood round the body. The same is true of us. Jesus said, *"I have come that they may have life, and have it to the full"* (John 10:10).

The implication is that until and unless we receive what Jesus has come to do, we aren't actually alive, at least not as God intends. We need an intervention. In fact, Jesus makes it clear that what's needed isn't a resuscitation but a new birth: *"flesh gives birth to flesh, but the Spirit gives birth to spirit"* (John 3:6). Being alive as God intends means being spiritually alive, and only he can bring us to that new birth.

Whether we're aware of that as a crisis experience (a conscious moment of conversion) or as the result of a process (where perhaps we can't name a date or time when we came to know God) becoming a Christian is an event. The starting point is the work of the Spirit bringing us from death to life, from darkness to light.

"You were dead in your transgressions and sins ... but because of his great love for us, God, who is rich in mercy, made us alive with Christ, even when we were dead in transgressions – it is by grace you have been saved." (Ephesians 2:1, 4-5)

But, having been born again, we need to grow up. Once

again, that is the work of the Spirit, who helps us grow into the family likeness. As I said in the introduction, I've come to recognise that this growth isn't linear, but instead involves a cycle of grace where we are continually being drawn into deeper relationship with God. John Wimber often used to say, "The way in is the way on." Spiritual growth seems to me to be circular, where we encounter the same truths in ever deepening ways, going on in our Christian lives by returning again and again to understand and experience them more profoundly. Since God deals with us individually, at any moment we'll each find that we're at a different point on the circle.

In describing how we grow as Christians, rather than how we become Christians, it's therefore impossible to talk as if we're all in the same place or pass through the same experiences. If there isn't one consistent path that's the same for everybody though, perhaps for many people spiritual growth really begins with the realisation of God's love for them personally. If we want to know how to "break into the circle" and consider our own spiritual growth, we could do no better than to start with the theme of intimacy with God. That may seem too personal or too intense for some of us to receive at this moment, but it's true. God loves us and he takes the initiative in drawing us deeper.

Our spiritual growth doesn't depend primarily on our effort, but on our response to the invitations and revelations that God – Father, Son and Holy Spirit – are longing to give. That's what "grace" means. Together, all three Persons of the Trinity work to draw us into *"the image and likeness"* of Jesus (Romans 8:29). As we've already seen, being like Jesus means so much more than imitating his character, and includes acting like him. But if Jesus is our model, how did Jesus do the things that he did?

We've already established that we cannot simply say "because he was God"; rather, his ministry was from his humanity, open to the Father's love and power. So it was something that could be modelled and passed on to his disciples, then and now.

Very little is said in the Bible about Jesus' childhood. We only have the stories of his conception and birth, of the flight to Egypt and return to Nazareth. Luke alone has a story about Jesus as a child, where he is separated from his parents because he remains in the Temple courts, amazing everyone with his understanding. The point of that incident appears to be that Jesus was always aware, at some level, of his relationship with the Father. Yet, that is all that we hear about Jesus' early years. To all intents and purposes, he lived an ordinary and unremarkable life as the carpenter's son (so it was thought). He lived amongst us, but performed no miracles as a child or young man.

The ministry of the adult Jesus begins with the announcement of his cousin, John the Baptist, that someone would come after him, who *"is more powerful than I, whose sandals I am not worthy to carry. He will baptise you with the*

Holy Spirit and fire" (Matthew 3:11). Immediately after this Jesus comes to John to be baptised, after which his ministry begins, in the power of the Holy Spirit. Only then do we start to hear of him demonstrating signs and wonders.

Looking at Matthew 3, at Jesus' baptism there are three things which are highlighted.

Firstly, his obedience to the Father is noted. John the Baptist understandably tried to deter Jesus from baptism – after all, John's baptism was a baptism of repentance. His role was to prepare the way for Jesus by calling the people back to God and pointing towards the one who would come after him. When he realised that Jesus was that One, how could he administer a baptism for the forgiveness of sins to the one who was sinless? Yet Jesus' answer is, *"Let it be so now; it is proper for us to do this to fulfil all righteousness"* (verse 15). The best way of understanding this verse is that the Lord is saying, "I am fully identifying with sinful humanity, entering completely into the Father's will." Jesus' obedience to the Father laid the foundation for the ministry he performed.

Secondly, he saw the Spirit come down, *"like a dove, and alighting on him"* (verse 16). In the Old Testament, doves were a symbol of innocence or purity, the sort of sacrifice that was commonplace for poor people (Leviticus 12:8). In the New Testament, Jesus only once speaks of doves, where he uses them as a symbol of gentleness (Matthew 10:16). Taken together, it seems that the manifestation of the Spirit

41

"like a dove" carries overtones of humility, as well as purity.

The Spirit isn't given for ostentation or showing off! Doves are also, by reputation, highly sensitive creatures. Unlike the bold pigeons of London, who are used to traffic and noises, doves are easily disturbed and will take flight if anything is wrong. Yet, the Spirit finds nothing wrong in Jesus. John later says, *"I saw the Spirit come down from heaven as a dove **and remain on him**"* (John 1:32). Perhaps that is a hint that everything was right about Jesus. Humility and holiness enabled Jesus to carry the Spirit's power permanently, without the Spirit ever being grieved.

Growing in obedience to the Father will help us receive more of the Spirit. Developing a more Christ-like character of humility and holiness will enable us to walk more consistently in his power. Yet, we need to remember that the Spirit is promised to us simply as a gift of grace. Jesus said, *"If you then, though you are evil, know how to give good gifts to your children, how much more will your Father in heaven give the Holy Spirit to those who ask him?"* (Luke 10:13). Nothing is mentioned about our earning the gift of the Spirit, or qualifying for him in any way except by being God's children. It's God's nature, as a good Father, to give us his Spirit.

That's why the third thing highlighted at Jesus' baptism is so important in learning to grow as a disciple: there was a voice from heaven which spoke and said, *"This is my Son, whom I love; with him I am well pleased"* (Matthew 3:17). It's receiving the Father's affirmation that so often is the key to releasing people into true discipleship.

I grew up with loving and supportive parents, but even with that heritage, I still found it hard as a Christian to comprehend how wonderful is God's grace to us, his children. I knew that God loved me, but struggled to grasp what it means for his love to be unconditional. It can't be earned, and in fact it can't be altered. Nothing I could ever do would be able to diminish it, or equally, increase it. God loves me because he loves me because he loves me. It's who he is, and he cannot do anything else but love his children. He doesn't wait for us to do anything before he showers us with favour – his delight is to see his children open themselves to all he has, because that shows that they know his true nature and trust him. The voice at Jesus' baptism said, *"This is my Son, whom I love; with him I am well pleased"* – and that was before Jesus had performed any miracles! Knowing God's love is the crucial foundation for growth in being like Jesus. With his Father, Jesus never had anything to hide, anything to prove or anything that he feared to lose. He could simply be available and share in what the Father was doing.

Many of us have not experienced the best human parenting. In adulthood, this can result in a fundamental insecurity, or in striving to earn the acceptance of important people in our lives. The reality is though, that none of us have experienced perfect parenting. Even the best human parents can only point us to God, who alone can meet those needs.

No family on earth will ever be so loving and so supportive that the children raised in it have no need of God! The role of the family is to be the place where the perfection of our Father in heaven is made intelligible so that ultimately we turn our lives towards him.

Before we seek to do ministry as disciples, we should realise what Jesus' baptism shows us. We work *from* the Father's affirmation, not *for* it! Just as the Lord had nothing to prove to his Father, nor do we. Our going out with him and serving others in his name is an act of worship, a response to his love, not an attempt to earn it. You cannot earn what is already freely given to you!

What we each need, in some form or other, is a revelation of God's love for us as individuals. Often this will come in the form of an encounter with his presence, as his love is never just an abstract idea. When we talk of "love" we don't mean that God simply expresses sentiments towards us from heaven; we mean that he moves towards us, with self-giving and sacrificial grace. Yet, we do also need to hear the words. Anyone who is married, or who is raising children, will know how important it is to actually say, *"I love you"* – and we all know how important it is to hear those words.

One of the songs that became an anthem at summer conferences in 2015 was *"Good, Good Father"*:

"I've heard a thousand stories
Of what they think You're like

But I've heard the tender whisper
Of love in the dead of night
And it tells me that You're pleased and
That I'm never alone.

You're a good, good Father,
It's who You are, who You are, who You are
And I'm loved by You
It's who I am, who I am, who I am."[2]

We constantly need that reminder. It is in God's very nature to love us and to shower us with affirmation. Quite simply, it's who he is. And our true nature is defined not by our experience of a human family, by the things that we've been through, or by the circumstances of our lives right now. Our true nature is defined by being the objects of his love. As the song says, "It's who I am."

Most Christians believe that God loves them, but few of us ever realise just *how much* he loves us. In all truth, we probably believe that God loves other people more than he loves us. Intellectually we might acknowledge that God has no favourites, and that we can't earn his love, but we still rebel against the idea of grace. The issue is that we instinctively respond that it's "too good to be true".

I remember grasping something of God's grace for myself once when I was on a plane. My wife Becky is from St Louis, Missouri, in the Midwest of America. We met when she came over to England for a term to study and found accommodation at Wycliffe Hall in Oxford, where I was training for ministry. Over the next couple of years, I took every opportunity to travel out to the States to see her but, being a student, was always taking the cheapest possible flights, sometimes changing planes three times.

Not really having flown before, I quickly became familiar with there being two different classes of people on an airplane, each having very different experiences. Those of us travelling on "second class" tickets were at the back of the plane. There was precious little leg-room, and the seats were narrow. In those days, the only entertainment in second-class was a film – no choice – on one small screen, shared by the whole cabin. Harassed stewardesses served basic drinks and unpalatable food, whereupon the person in front often seemed to decide it was time to sleep and reclined their seat almost into your tray.

Overall, it was definitely not a pleasant experience. However, if you were seated in an aisle seat, something else became apparent. From time to time, one of the stewards would pull back a curtain and you would glimpse another world! Beyond the curtain was the world of "first class"... and everything was better. Stewards were serving a choice of drinks. Each passenger had a roomy seat that could even recline into a bed. There was an individual choice of entertainment. (Sometimes, when I tell this story now, I mention that you could see a pig being cooked, rotating slowly on a spit as some of the passengers played badminton, however that is probably too fanciful...!). Everything in you longed to be in that cabin.

Imagine being on a plane like that, but hearing an unusual message over the intercom. "Ladies and Gentleman, this is your Captain speaking. We have a very unique situation on our plane today. We have very few people onboard and none of our first class passengers have turned up, so we would like to invite all of our passengers to come forward and enjoy all the amenities of first class." What would be your reaction? Most likely, different people would react in different ways. Some people would have no hesitation. Many would turn to their neighbour, seeking reassurance that it actually was alright to go forward. I can imagine also though, that there would be some who would refuse to go. "I can't go. I have my ticket here, and my ticket says 'second-class.'"

It's an exaggerated and silly example, but it touches a nerve for many people. It also comes very close to the spiritual truth of what Jesus did for us on the cross. The Bible says that in the Temple there was a curtain separating the people from the Holy of Holies, the very presence of God. Only the High Priest could enter behind that curtain, and only once a year, to offer a sacrifice on behalf of the people. Yet, when Jesus died, the curtain was torn from top to bottom, from heaven to earth, to tell us that the way into God's presence is wide open (Matthew 27:51). There are no first- and second-class Christians; all are loved equally. His arms are wide open and he's waiting for us to run to him.

As I've spoken on Matthew 3:17 over the past couple of years, I've realised that the Father wants to say the exact same words over each of his children. He longs for each of us to hear these words for ourselves, from him. I've often divided the time of prayer afterwards into two, so that women can hear me say to them, in the Father's name, "You are my daughter, whom I love; with you I am well pleased," and men hear, "You are my son...". Those times of prayer have frequently been powerful and healing. Many women have spoken to me about their need to hear themselves addressed as "daughter", when our English bibles often subsumes their gender within a generic "sons" for all God's children. They've spoken of how much pressure they feel under to live up to a standard set by the world, reinforced by glossy magazines and airbrushed images. Knowing that their Father calls them "daughter" and declares them "well-pleasing" has been liberating.

Yet, if anything, it has been the times of prayer ministry with men which have been most revealing. We still have a generation alive whose parenting was Victorian – in its values, if not directly – and subsequent generations have further been crippled by a false "macho" idea of masculinity. Many men labour under the crushing burden of having to prove themselves to an earthly father, boss or superior officer. Even when no such figure exists in their history, somehow our culture has left them feeling that they need to prove themselves to themselves, in order to be a "real man".

Some of those most affected by receiving the words, "You are my son, whom I love; with you I am well pleased" have been older people, with some saying that they had never heard them spoken over their lives in sixty or seventy years. I was reminded of a deeply moving letter that Rob Parsons once received from a lady, which he mentions in *The Sixty Minute Marriage*:

"I was a disappointment to my father. He wanted a son. He never hugged me, praised me, or told me he loved me. I realise he was a product of his generation and I have forgiven him, but my self-esteem is very low. I am often depressed and I am riddled with guilt. I am eighty-five years old".[3]

The absence of affirmation from an earthly father can cause a lifetime of emotional pain, insecurity and lack of confidence. The good news for us all is that receiving the affirmation of our heavenly father has an even greater effect in a positive direction. It enables us to walk in boldness, to allow the promises in his word to become the bedrock and defining reality in every circumstance, and with full assurance of his presence in our lives at every moment. The truth is that God does indeed love you as much as he has ever loved anyone.

You will never grow tired of hearing God's voice of love speaking to you, nor will you or I ever come to a place where we don't need to hear it any more. We will have to come back to this truth again and again. Some of us are, by nature, activists – I certainly am! – people who are never happier than when we are going out and doing things with the Lord. All of us, but activists especially perhaps, need to remember that Jesus' pattern for discipleship begins with the rhythm of "being with him" as well as being "sent out" (Mark 3:14). It's when we're intimate with God that we are able to hear these words of affirmation; and that is when we can take the next step in spiritual growth, which is understanding our identity as his sons and daughters.

Notes

1. Quoted in John Stott's last sermon, delivered at the Keswick Convention, July 17, 2007.
2. *Good Good Father*, Pat Barrett and Anthony Brown of the band Housefires.
3. Rob Parsons, *The Sixty Minute Marriage*, Hodder & Stoughton, 1997, p49.

4
Affirmation leads to identity

As a species, we are in the grip of a profound identity crisis. There is an old joke that goes something like this:

At the airport, a crowded flight was cancelled. A single airline customer agent was trying to rebook a long line of frustrated and inconvenienced travellers.

Suddenly an angry passenger pushed his way to the desk. He slapped his ticket down on the counter and said, "I HAVE to be on this flight and it HAS to be FIRST CLASS." The agent replied, "I'm sorry sir. I'll be happy to help you, but I've got to help all these other people first, then I'm sure we'll be able to work something out."

The passenger was unimpressed. He asked loudly, so that the passengers behind him could hear, "Do you have any idea WHO I AM?"

Without hesitating, the gate agent smiled and grabbed

her public address microphone. *"May I have your attention please?"* she began, her voice bellowing throughout the terminal. *"We have a passenger here at the gate WHO HAS FORGOTTEN WHO HE IS. If anyone can help, please come to the gate."*

As a race, we have forgotten who we really are.

Since we were created by God and for God, we will never be truly satisfied until we are back in relationship with him. He made us in his image, so deep within our nature is the desire to be connected to him again. When Jesus said, *"I have come that they might have life, and have it to the full"* (John 10:10), what that means is that, until and unless we allow him to change things, we are not truly living. If he has come to "bring life", then clearly that life must be lacking. What we call "life" is, for many people, merely existing. I wonder whether the fascination in recent years in popular TV shows, computer games and films, with zombies and the "walking dead" reveals a deep sense in our culture that we're merely "going through the motions" rather than actually being alive.

Humanity cannot live without God. We can explain so much, build great structures, achieve incredible technological advances, and yet experience increasing levels of dissatisfaction and depression. All because we were never intended to live apart from God himself. The great Christian thinker G.K. Chesterton was writing about this as far back as the turn of the 20th century.

In his book, *Orthodoxy*, written in 1908, Chesterton points out the weaknesses of the rational, scientific, materialist worldview – the way that most of us have been trained to look at the world, that is, without reference to the spiritual dimension. One of Chesterton's assertions is that fairy stories, where miraculous things can happen, are often more true than works that reduce everything to that which can be explained. At root, he says, people are unhappy because they have forgotten our relationship to the invisible God, our Creator, and of being made in his image:

"We have all read in scientific books and, indeed, in all romances, the story of the man who has forgotten his name. This man walks about the streets and can see and appreciate everything; only he cannot remember who he is. Well, every man is that man in the story. Every man has forgotten who he is ... We are all under the same mental calamity; we have all forgotten our names. We have all forgotten who and what we really are. All that we call common sense and rationality and practicality and positivism only means that for certain dead levels of our life we forget that we have forgotten. All that we call spirit and art and ecstasy only means that for one awful instant we remember that we forget."[1]

Life is a miracle. So the most important things in life – truth, beauty, justice, love, for example – can't be fully explained and must instead be experienced. All those things are, in fact, embodied in Jesus and so we know them ultimately through developing a relationship with him. More than that though, and even more essential than being able to appreciate life, Jesus brings us into his relationship with the Father, so that we too become his children.

"See what great love the Father has lavished on us, that we should be called children of God! And that is what we are!" (1 John 3:1)

We talked in the last chapter about experiencing God's love for us as individuals. A genuine encounter with God's love will always lead to the revelation of God's affirmation, but it will also show us who we really are. John Wesley, the founder of Methodism and leader of the great revival of the eighteenth century in this country, had been in ordained ministry for a whole decade before he experienced this. He had travelled to the mission field in America, but his ministry had largely been a failure and he returned to England.

It was only in 1738, ten years after ordination, that Wesley attended a meeting of which he said, "In the evening I went very unwillingly to a society in Aldersgate Street, where one was reading Luther's Preface to the Epistle to the Romans. About a quarter before nine, while he was describing the change which God works in the heart through faith in Christ, I felt my heart strangely warmed. I felt I did trust in Christ, Christ alone for salvation, and an assurance was given me that he had taken away my sins, even mine, and saved me from the law of sin and death."[2]

What Wesley encountered was God's love for him personally, a gift of grace rather than reward for merit. He only discovered this after a decade of strict holiness, piety and toil, all service undertaken as duty rather than joy. It was when he came to the end of his own resources, as it has been for so many of us since, that he was able to understand and receive grace. Reflecting on this later, Wesley described the change as "exchanging the faith of a servant ... for the faith of a son."[3] His ministry was never the same, because his relationship with the Father was no longer that of a servant. Knowing God's affirmation always leads to a deeper revelation of our true identity as his sons and daughters.

All of us have the experience of being a child. Our parents' role was to help us develop into mature and healthy adults though, rather than keep us as immature children. Most parents understand instinctively that you do that through a combination of unconditional love and spoken affirmation – exactly what we've seen God our Father does for us. That shouldn't be a surprise when you consider that God our Father defines what our "parent/child" relationships should be, not the other way round. When we say that God is our Father, and we are his children, that isn't an illustration! It is the deepest truth of our lives as Christians, and something we must learn to live out.

In 2015, Becky and I were asked to go over to Jersey to speak at the New Wine Channel Islands annual conference. Jersey is a beautiful island so this was no hardship, and it was a very encouraging time. The theme of the conference was "Fearless", based on 1 John 4:18: *"perfect love drives out fear."* So, having been asked to speak on that theme, I thought I would check to see from which fears the love of the Lord delivers us!

Could we claim that promise in our struggles with spiders, for instance, or perhaps with deeper fears such as the fear of being overwhelmed by life, or of losing loved ones? If you have even a minor phobia, there is good news – I'm sure that the Lord wants to heal us of anything that negatively affects our enjoyment of life. In fact, I learnt from some reading that, as babies, we are only born with two fears – loud noises and falling backwards – and develop all other fears later, based on life experiences. The healing of our memories should deal with most of those phobias!

In context though, that verse has a much more focussed reference. *"There is no fear in love. But perfect love drives out fear, because fear has to do with punishment. The one who fears is not made perfect in love."* The specific fear is that of being punished, of being on the wrong side of judgment. In other words, it is the fear that God will find something against you. To be made perfect in love is to know God so well that you would never fear punishment.

Confirming that reading of the text is the preceding verse.

The whole section is a reflection on God's love, and especially on how he has shown that love to us by sending Jesus as *"an atoning sacrifice for our sins"* (1 John 4:10), but it works up to a breathtaking statement that should probably be far better known than verse 18! 1 John 4:17 says, *"This is how love is made complete among us so that we have confidence on the day of judgment: In this world we are like Jesus."*

None of us would normally lay claim to being like Jesus! It sounds arrogant – and it would be if we were claiming that we were as morally good or as powerfully used by God as him. We are always aware, sometimes painfully so, of how far short we fall from the example that Jesus gives us. What can happen though, is that humility tips over into a denial of being like Jesus in any way. Far too often, the gospels have been read as if Jesus was so different, so unlike us, that we could never aspire to be like him. Yet, discipleship involves becoming like your Master. We are indeed meant to become like Jesus – because he shows us what it is to be truly human (without ever ceasing to be truly God).

A Christian is someone who is like Jesus, and who over time, led by the Spirit, becomes more like him. The title, "Christ", is the Greek translation of Hebrew terms with rich history, but simply means "anointed one". So "Christians" are little "anointed ones" – we share the same Spirit that empowered Jesus and by whom he did such wonderful things. We can, if we only had the faith to believe it, be like

Jesus in any situation ... because we have the same access to heaven's resources.

The basis for that bold claim is that we too are children of God. Jesus is the only-begotten Son, uniquely the Son from eternity, but we are also sons and daughters. That's the main thrust of 1 John, as John deals with false teaching. He wants the Church to know who they are, and all that is therefore theirs through Christ.

"In this world we are like him" because the Father loves us just as much as he loves Jesus. We don't deserve it, of course, but that is the grace and generosity of a God who is the very definition of love. We know it's the case because he has given us his Spirit to live inside us. God the Father doesn't withhold things from us – he makes the same resources available to us as he did to Jesus. Love and power go together. We just struggle to believe how much we are loved, and so to accept how much comes with that love.

It must have been hard for Kate Middleton, a "commoner" (as they say), to embrace her new identity when she married and became Catherine, Duchess of Cambridge. The world that the Royal Family inhabits is not one that anyone outside the family would have experienced before. Suddenly having to think of a palace as "my home" surely takes some doing! There must be many trappings of royalty that would feel awkward for someone who was not born to them, or that would make them feel self-conscious. And in the same manner, few of us grasp when we come into a relationship with God that being loved as his children includes access to his presence (and thereby his power) in a new way as well.

It's the Spirit's role to retrain our minds and hearts to believe this.

In Galatians 4, Paul says that Jesus has redeemed us from being unable to keep the Law, *"that we might receive the full rights of sons"* (Galatians 4:5). Not "some rights" but "the full rights". God holds nothing good back from his children. *"Because you are sons* (and daughters), *God sent the Spirit of his Son into our hearts, the Spirit who calls out, 'Abba, Father'"* (verse 6). The Spirit's voice in us is an inner witness to our new and true identity. God is our Father and we are indeed his children. *"So you are no longer a slave but a son; and since you are a son, God has made you also an heir"* (verse 7).

In Romans 8, Paul puts it in a similar way:

"Those who are led by the Spirit are the sons of God. For you did not receive a spirit that makes you a slave again to fear, but rather the Spirit you received brought about your adoption to sonship. And by him we cry, 'Abba, Father'. The Spirit himself testifies with our spirit that we are God's children. Now if we are children, then we are heirs – heirs of God and co-heirs with Christ." (Romans 8:14-17).

Now that we are God's children, fear is an inappropriate way of responding to him. The "fear of the Lord" mentioned in Proverbs is more about respect and honour than abject terror. God is never to be treated lightly or taken for granted, but neither is he to be avoided or become an object of dread to his children. Seeing God as he really is means bowing down in worship; but knowing who we are means boldly coming to him with expectation.

Being "co-heirs with Christ" points to what we receive when he comes again and we get to share in his glory. There is a great reward stored up for the faithful. But remember the implications for this present age as well. *"In this world, we are like him"* (1 John 4:17). We are loved by God, and he is with us just as he was with Jesus.

I think that sometimes we want to hide behind phrases such as, "Of course ... that was Jesus", as if somehow God treats us as lesser children. Obviously Jesus is different from us in many ways: as the one who has always been the Son – being perfect in all that he did, without sin; and fully understanding his identity – but that doesn't mean that God loves us any less. I can't find anything in the Bible that says that God loves us with a love different from that which he has for Jesus. Deep down in my heart I feel that there *should* be such a statement, but perhaps that says more about our inability to understand the breathtaking quality of God's grace.

Adopted children have no less status as children in a family than those born naturally. We'll think more on that in the next chapter, but let's remember that the central truth is God's affection for us. When the Bible talks about us being adopted into God's family, as in the Romans quote above, we are not to hear that we are anything other than fully loved sons and daughters. In one sense, we should simply revel in the grace of adoption – after all, there are no accidental adoptions! No one wakes up in the morning to discover that they have an additional and unexpected new member of the family. Watching friends go through the process of adoption, I've seen how much is involved. It's a costly and emotional process of preparation and training, but in the end it comes down to a parent saying to a child, "I choose you to become my child." And, from what I've observed afterwards, those adopted children are loved as much as those who were born into the family.

As I was writing this chapter, I came across one of the new songs by Amanda Cook from Bethel. These are words that capture the wonder of our new identity as sons and daughters of God:

"My past embraced
My sin forgiven
I'm blameless in Your sight
My history rewritten.

You delight in showing mercy
Mercy triumphs over judgment.

Oh Love, great Love
Fear cannot be found in You
There will never be a day

You're uncertain of the ones You choose."[4]

You are, and always will be, a child of God – and he will never regret making that choice to bring you into his family.

Notes

1. G.K. Chesterton, *Orthodoxy*, ch4, The Ethics of Elfland.
2. Journal of John Wesley, VI.II.XVI.
3. John Wesley, *Sermons on Several Occasions*, London 1851, p356.
4. *Mercy* by Amanda Cook, from the Bethel album *Brave New World*, Integrity Music, 2015.

5
Identity leads to authority

This is a record of an interesting radio exchange that is supposed to have taken place at sea:

This is the US Navy. You are directly in our path. Alter your course ten points to the north.

This is the Spanish Navy. You alter your course ten points to the north.

I am an Admiral. Alter your course ten points to the north.

I am an Able Seaman. You alter your course ten points to the north.

I am a battleship. Alter your course ten points to the north.

I am a lighthouse. It's your choice!

Knowing who you are gives you great authority! It would be fair to say that even those of us who are comfortable confessing our identity as sons and daughters of God can be hesitant in claiming the rights that the Bible says come with that identity. Even more significantly perhaps, we don't appreciate the spiritual authority carried by Princes and Princesses in service to the King of Kings. Our ability to advance the Kingdom of God naturally depends on whether we know and can exercise the authority that we have been given.

One of Paul's most interesting letters is that written to the Galatians. This wasn't, it appears, a church of people who were immoral or irreligious – on the contrary, they seem desperate to be right with God – but Paul speaks some of the harshest words in the New Testament to them. He is astonished that they have turned their back on the gospel as he preached it, and instead are allowing themselves to be influenced by other preachers, whose message is filled with legalism rather than grace. He reminds them of their initial experience of Jesus, how they were saved and experienced the Spirit's power when they knew they didn't deserve anything, simply as a gift of God's grace. Yet, now they wanted additional reassurance through outward signs of being right with God, such as circumcision and keeping the Jewish Law.

Whilst we might not relate to any temptation to embrace the Law of Moses, we probably can relate to the feeling that we need to do something more in order to remain loved by God. It's so easy to turn what started out as a relationship into something that becomes essentially "rules based". Paul's point is that, since Jesus came, we have the opportunity of a completely new standing with God, through faith in his Son.

"Before the coming of this faith, we were held in custody under the Law, locked up until the faith that was to come would be revealed. So the Law was our guardian until Christ came that we might be justified by faith. Now that this faith has come, we are no longer under a guardian." (Galatians 3:23-25)

What gives us this new status is that *"in Christ Jesus, you are children of God through faith"* (verse 26). All that matters is our identity as God's children, not where we have come from or what the world might say about us. *"There is neither Jew nor Gentile, neither slave nor free, nor is there male or female, for you are all one in Christ Jesus"* (verse 28). By this, Paul doesn't mean that human distinctions no longer exist – of course people still have different racial backgrounds, different social circumstances, and different genders – but these things are irrelevant when it comes to who can enjoy the status of *"child of God"* – and receive the benefits of that name. What is required is that we realise the identity we now have.

By turning back to the Law, the Galatians were living as if Jesus had not come. They weren't seemingly able to comprehend a relationship with God as their Father, instead choosing to approach him as someone whose love was conditional. Paul's response is that, since Jesus came, everything has changed.

"What I am saying is that as long as an heir is underage, he is no different from a slave, although he owns the whole estate. The heir is subject to guardians and trustees until the time set by his father. So also, when we were underage, we were in slavery ... But when the set time had fully come, God sent his Son ... to redeem those under the Law, that we might receive adoption to sonship." (Galatians 4:1-5)

Children in that culture had to live under the care of a guardian until they were recognised as adults. They had no rights and no freedoms until they were deemed old enough to take their rightful place. Think of coming from a rich family and having a trust fund of many millions of pounds. Until the "set time" comes, you cannot access it and are effectively as poor as everyone else. The point of this passage though is that the time has now come! It's time to enjoy the inheritance that comes with the identity.

The word that is translated here as "adoption to sonship" refers to a specific ceremony which would have been familiar to all of Paul's first readers. Literally translated, the word that Paul uses means "son placement". It was when the father determined that it was time for his male heir to pass from being a child (under the care of guardians and under the absolute authority of the father) to being fully legally vested with all of the rights, powers and privileges of being a son and heir to his father's possessions, wealth and status. No longer was he viewed as a child – he was a full, participating member of his society and family. If this ceremony was performed for a child born outside the family – what we normally mean when we say "adoption" today – then the old life of the adoptee was completely erased and all previous obligations cancelled. The child would, in every sense, have a new father and be co-heir with any natural offspring.

More than that though, the now-adult son was legally empowered to act in the father's business. The father was publicly affirming the son as someone empowered to act in his name. In the ceremony was also a transfer of authority. The father would take the son and acknowledge him as his own – "this is my son, whom I love" – so that everyone would know that the son was authorised to run the family business. With our "adoption to sonship" comes a commissioning from God our Father. Just as he spoke over his eternal Son at his baptism, the Father speaks over us who have become his children through faith. So, receiving the words of affirmation – "This is my son/this is my daughter, whom I love, with whom I am well pleased!" – isn't simply an experience of love but also of trust. God our Father is saying to us, "I trust you, I believe in you, and I will back you up as you step out in my name. All the resources of my house are now at your disposal, and I am sending you also to be about my business."

Satan trembles when any one of us understands being a child of God in those terms. It shouldn't surprise us therefore that the primary focus of spiritual warfare for the

Christian is around the issue of identity. If the enemy can stop us from coming to a proper understanding of being God's sons and daughters – so that we don't realise what is available to us and act like sons and daughters – then he can render us ineffective. I often think of it in this way: once we've come to know Jesus, Satan can't stop us from going to heaven (remember that Jesus said that no one can snatch us out of his hand, John 10:28), therefore he changes his tactics and focuses instead on making sure we don't take anyone else with us when we go!

When God calls us to be his sons and daughters, it means not only that he is restoring us in relationship, but he's also commissioning us to be part of his plan of salvation for others. We join his family, we start to take on the family likeness ... and we get involved in the family business. We find a fresh and fulfilling purpose in revealing him to others.

I once heard an American preacher describe it in a particularly memorable way. He said,

"The best thing you can do for a Christian is baptise them and shoot them!"

I think what he meant was, once someone has become a Christian and is secure in that relationship, the best thing that they could ever experience is life with the Father in glory. Think of it – what could be better than life with God in his perfect heaven? Yet we're still down here in this broken world. Why would a loving Father make us stay any longer than we have to in a world that's marred by sin, evil and pain? The only answer must be that there is still work for us to do here...

That's actually a good unpacking of what Paul says in Philippians 1:21-24. Sitting in prison and thinking that he is facing his own imminent death, Paul says that he's comforted by the knowledge that *"to me, to live is Christ and to die is gain"* (verse 21). Dying would mean going to be with Jesus, which is *"better by far"* (verse 23), but remaining alive means more opportunity for ministry (which would be better for others). While we are here on earth, we have a purpose in God's plan for others. As Craig Groeschel puts it, "If you aren't dead, you aren't done".[1]

However, if you don't know who you truly are, you won't realise the authority that belongs to you and won't be able to fulfil God's purpose for your life. What difference would it make to our ability to resist temptation if we knew for certain that we were children of the King? What could earth offer that would be better than what is already ours? Or how much might it affect our prayer life if we were 100% confident that we genuinely are God's children, and are therefore bringing our requests to a loving heavenly Father with the full assurance of children that he loves to lavish good things on us? Living in a manner worthy of our calling, praying with confidence – as well as resisting doubts, refusing low self-esteem, rejecting the enemy's lies, and many other things – all come from knowing our true identity.

Spiritual warfare is much simpler, yet more subtle, than

we often make it out to be. On the whole, it takes place in our minds, as Satan tries to deceive us, seduce us, or send us to sleep. He uses lies and half-truths to undermine our confidence in God and our awareness of who we are in him. As Robby Dawkins has written recently, Satan isn't just an identity thief, who blinds you to who you are, "he convinces you that you are someone other than who you really are."[2] He takes away the knowledge of our true identity AND tries to give us a false (lesser) one, usually rooted in shame and guilt.

Our experience as God's children is naturally going to echo that of Jesus, our brother and model. It's worth noting that the very first thing that happens after Jesus' baptism, where you'll recall that the Father's voice from heaven spoke affirmation over him, was that he was *led by the Spirit into the desert to be tempted by the devil*" (Matthew 4:1). That it was the Spirit who led him there seems to suggest that this had to happen.

It isn't possible to emerge as a servant of God without going through a battle. Satan's temptation of Jesus involved three things: satisfy your body by turning stones into bread, reassure your ego by making the angels catch you when you jump off the pinnacle of the temple, and take a shortcut to your mission by compromising in worship.

People interpret those temptations in various ways, but what they all have in common is this: Jesus is being attacked around the issue of his identity. Every time Satan tries to tempt Jesus, he begins with the words, "If you are the Son of God..."[3] In other words, he is planting subtle seeds of doubt and requiring Jesus to prove his identity to reassure himself! (After all, Satan knows full well who Jesus is). By answering with scripture each time, Jesus is refusing to play that game. For him, as it should be for us, it is enough that *"it is written."* He needs no further reassurance than the promise of God.

We read in Luke 4:1 that Jesus was *"full of the Holy Spirit"* when he went into the desert; but after the test it says, *"Jesus returned to Galilee **in the power of the Spirit**"* (Luke 4:14) and began to preach and perform miracles. If we discern a change there, then perhaps that reveals the wisdom of the Spirit in leading Jesus into that test. Even as the only-begotten, eternal Son of the Father, Jesus' identity was tested before his ministry. That was part of the process of manifesting that identity and taking up the commission that comes with it.

I spent a long time, as many people do, not able to accept that "it is written" with regard to things the Bible said about me. As I began to believe it though, the things of the Kingdom – praying for people in the power of the Spirit, hearing God's voice, knowing that God was somehow powerfully working through me – these things came more easily.

In a prayer meeting recently, our curate James shared a picture that spoke to me about this. In his mind, he saw a plane with vertical take-off and landing capabilities (VTOL), rather like the famous Harrier jump jets used by the British Navy and Air Force (amongst others). Instinctively, people expect planes to need a long runway in order to take off, but these planes were designed in such a way that they could fly in and out of forest clearings, or from the decks of ships. I realised that we often think of being effective in Kingdom ministry in similar terms. Who will God use to perform signs and wonders? Our gut reaction, whether we make an explicit theology of it or not, is that you need to be a mature Christian, someone who has taken time to get to know God well, maybe even earned his favour.

On reflection, we probably communicate that we believe exactly that through many things that we say. Children need to learn to walk after all, and we certainly believe that we need to grow as Christians. Yet, the moment you become a Christian, you receive the Holy Spirit. There is no reason why you can't take off immediately. God could use the prayers of the most recent convert to accomplish his will. He uses those who are available, not only those who are mature.

In 2012, I met one young woman who "took off" immediately. It was the year of the London Olympics and our church, just a few miles from Stratford, hosted several mission teams over the twelve months. Amy was part of a Youth with a Mission (YWAM) team, and led her group out to the streets of Ilford nearby. This was a very multi-cultural area and, as they set up signs offering prayer and began worshipping, quickly a crowd of Sikh men gathered.

She was, however, disappointed that none seemed to want prayer, so Amy left the group and went in search of someone with whom she could pray.

Rounding a corner she ran, literally, into a small Pakistani man, and heard God tell her that he was the one. This man's name was Saqib, although she was frustrated to find out that he was already a Christian, one of the small minority of Pakistani Christians. But, she reasoned, even though she was keen for people who *didn't* know God to experience his power and love, praying for Saqib was certainly a good thing to do – and he was instantly healed of pain in his neck and shoulder. Being overwhelmed by this experience, Saqib asked to know more about healing, so Amy invited him to join their team and, with a friend, took him to a local café to explain their approach.

Whilst in the middle of this training, one of the Sikh men from the crowd entered and wanted to ask them questions. He managed to communicate that his name was Dadir, that he had been drawn to their worship, and that he was impressed that they were not asking for money. Something in him recognised the God for whom he longed and he wanted to know more about Jesus. Amy and her friend began to tell him about Jesus, but frequently struggled to get past Dadir's poor English.

At this point, Saqib interjected and asked, "Do you speak Punjabi?" God had provided the interpreter! The conversation became much easier and Dadir responded so enthusiastically that Amy's friend said to her, "I think he wants to become a Christian!" Having had some training in evangelism amongst people of other faiths, Amy responded that Dadir might just be saying that he would recognise Jesus alongside the other gurus that he revered. Nevertheless, she spoke to him about Jesus being uniquely *"the way, the truth and the life"* (John 14:6), and his call on us to renounce all other gods. To her surprise, Dadir excitedly agreed and, there and then, she led him in a prayer of commitment, through Saqib's translation, and left him with a Bible.

The next day, the team returned to the same spot to find a crowd already gathered. At the centre of the group was Dadir, reading from the Bible and speaking to the Sikh men. Sidling up to a man at the edge of the crowd, Amy asked what Dadir was saying.

"Oh, he's telling us about Jesus," said the man.

"Yes, he gave his life to Jesus yesterday," she replied.

"No, you don't understand ... we revere many religious teachers; he will just have added Jesus to them," came the response.

Amy patiently explained what had taken place the day before, and how they had talked about that very thing, and insisted that the man ask Dadir. When the man heard Dadir's answer, he turned back to Amy in shock.

"He says that he believes that Jesus is the only way, and that we should all believe in him. Do you know what this means? This man is our local teacher – and he's saying that he must now go to the central Temple in London to explain that he can no longer be our leader".

Amy replied, "Well then, things are going to change for all of you!"

A year later I met Saqib, who told me that he and Dadir had both joined Asian fellowships. A number of Sikh men have been converted and baptised through Dadir's witness. All this through the confident faith and boldness of one young woman making herself available to God and stepping out in faith.

Amy had only been a Christian for about a year. Many people would love to be part of a story like that, but after decades in church still think that they are somehow lacking.

I've seen it many times. People join the Alpha course and, ten weeks later, have been thoroughly converted, filled with the Spirit, spoken in tongues and are regularly praying for the sick to be healed. Do they still need to grow in the fruits of the Spirit and in Christian maturity? Of course. But, if they grasp the authority that comes with their new identity as a child of God, then they can jump right into the supernatural. And often, they seem to understand discipleship better than people who have been in church for decades.

You don't have to strive to become who you are. Simply accept who God declares you to be, and pick up that authority.

Notes

1. *Generational Tension*, Craig Groeschel, Willow Creek Global Leaders Summit talk, 2010.
2. Robby Dawkins, *Identity Thief*, Chosen Books, 2015, p17.
3. In Matthew 4, the third temptation doesn't explicitly use those words. However, in Luke's version of the Temptation of Jesus (Luke 4) they are Satan's first words in each of the three temptations.

6
Authority leads to destiny

At this point it might be worth taking stock of what we've said so far. From the beginning, Jesus sought to involve his disciples in the ministry of the Kingdom. He modelled something for us as a human being, operating in the power of the Holy Spirit. God's plan for his Church is, and always has been, for a people who display his character and are available to be used by his power. Learning to live in that supernatural way is the essence of growth as a disciple; it means becoming more like Jesus, not just in his character but also in the way that God used him.

For many of us that seems unattainable though. We find ourselves lacking faith or bound up by all sorts of fears. However, by co-operating with the work of the Holy Spirit, we can grow into all that God has for us. The Spirit fills us with God's love and gives us that foundational sense of being secure. He enables us to hear the Father's voice of affirmation and encouragement. In return, he inspires in us a love for God that helps us embrace our identity as sons and daughters so that we can approach God with confidence. And, as we learn to explore the inheritance of the children of God, the Spirit gives us authority in the spiritual realm. The question now is, will we take it up and use it?

There is an old legend that has been attached to the story of Alexander the Great. Supposedly, after one of his many campaigns, a young soldier was brought before him accused of cowardice. When Alexander the Great asked the name of the soldier, he was told that he too was called Alexander. The great warrior's response was to call the young man before him, look him in the eye and simply say, "Change your name or change your nature."

Most of us have an interest in names. If you have children it's likely that you will have chosen their names carefully. They might be names that have passed down through your family, which you have chosen to honour. You may simply like the sound of the name and think it sounds pretty or interesting; you will almost certainly have looked up the meaning of the name though. In the Bible, people's names carry huge significance. Sometimes they describe that person's nature. Other times they witness to what God has done.

That isn't always the case though. As I said, I met my wife Becky when I was a student at theological college and she was a lodger staying in one of the college's spare rooms. When you have a biblical name it's always dangerous to be around people who are studying theology. The gifts in most card shops will tell you that "Rebecca" means "captivating"; so she wasn't too impressed when I passed on my discovery that Rebecca (the biblical spelling is "Rebekah") comes from the Hebrew meaning "a short length of rope for tying up goats"! Of course, my own name, "Paul", simply means "small" so I didn't have a leg to stand on. It's never felt particularly flattering compared to the meaning of most other people's names, although I have grown to love the biblical Paul. So, it was with some interest a few years ago that I started to ask myself when Paul actually became "Paul". After all, he is introduced to us first in the Book of Acts as "Saul", and remains so for several chapters.

I had always assumed that it was simply an expression of Paul's humility that he eventually adopted his new name. Listening to Rowan Williams, however, in his Lent lectures during his time as Archbishop of Canterbury, cast things in a somewhat different light for me. In Jewish tradition, Saul was an honoured name. Despite the weaknesses of the Old Testament character, the tribe of Benjamin took great pride in having produced Israel's first King – a pride that Paul shared (Philippians 3:5). In Greek, however, things are quite different. Rowan Williams suggested that Saul may have changed his name because the Greek transliteration ("Saulos") had the unfortunate meaning of "the sultry walk of a prostitute"! (That would be quite a barrier for a preacher with an important message. Imagine sitting in a synagogue and trying to take seriously a guest speaker called Rabbi Bootylicious...).

Whatever the reason behind Saul's name change, and why he chose the name Paul, I started looking into when it happened and have come to see that it is another significant step in Paul's own spiritual journey. When we first meet Paul (then known as Saul) he is a persecutor of the Church in Acts 7:58 and 8:1-3. Chapter 9 tells us of Paul's conversion experience and his initial ministry as a preacher (Acts 9:20f). Whilst the focus of the Book of Acts then shifts back to Peter, it seems from evidence in the epistles that Paul's next few years include time in Arabia, a visit to Jerusalem, followed by a return to his native town of Tarsus. It's from there that Barnabas calls him across to Antioch to help teach and disciple those converted in the first intentional outreach to non-Jews. Whenever he is mentioned though, it is always as "Barnabas and Saul" – always "Saul" and always second. What I discovered was that Saul's change of name is inextricably linked with him stepping into the fullness of his own personal destiny.

We shouldn't minimise just how much Paul was already doing. He had already experienced a personal encounter with the Lord, been filled with the Holy Spirit and healed of blindness. He had been preaching for a number of years with boldness and great authority. So powerful had been his witness that several times already he had had his life threatened and had been forced to withdraw. Paul was already a serious preacher as "Saul, the converted Jew", but there was a fuller expression or realisation of his identity into which, at this point, he had not yet stepped. I believe that is the case for many of us. Growth comes from our decision to take our identity from God, rather than from our backgrounds or our circumstances. Despite the fact that we're all called to become like Jesus, becoming all that God intends is a unique call for us all.

On a visit to our church once, Bishop Stephen Cottrell said, "When I stand before God, he is not going to ask me, 'Why didn't you become like Billy Graham?' Or 'Why didn't you become like Mother Teresa?' He might ask me though, 'Why didn't you become the Stephen Cottrell that I intended?'"

It's only in Acts chapter 13 that Saul the converted Jew becomes "Paul the Apostle" and the man that I believe God had called him to be. In Acts chapter 13:2, the Holy Spirit spoke to the Antioch church and initiated what would become known as Paul's first missionary journey. *"While they were worshipping the Lord and fasting, the Holy Spirit said, 'Set apart from me Barnabas and Saul for the work to which I have called them.'"* (Again, note, always named "Saul" and always named second).

Bible scholars usually say that in the spring of AD47 Barnabas and Saul began the first missionary journey making their first focus Cyprus – Barnabas' home country.

We read that they preached in the Jewish synagogues and travelled through the whole island until they came to Paphos. Clearly what they were doing was causing quite a stir in the local community; so much so that the proconsul, Sergius Paulus, the ruler of the island, called for them *"because he wanted to hear the word of God"* (Acts 13:7).

It isn't hard to imagine that what might be at stake in an encounter with such an influential person is nothing less than the spiritual future of the island. Naturally, therefore, there is immediately spiritual opposition (verse 8) and a power encounter (verse 9f). Sergius Paulus was attended by a Jewish sorcerer and false prophet called Bar-Jesus, also known by the Greek name Elymas (which simply means "sorcerer"). We read that he *"opposed them and tried to turn the proconsul from the faith."*

The Jewish name Bar-Jesus wasn't a reference to Christ, as Jesus was a common name, but literally meant "Son of the Saviour". In reality, of course, he was nothing of the sort. This however is the first time that we hear of Saul having another name.

"Then Saul, who was also called Paul, filled with the Holy Spirit, looked straight at Elymas and said, 'You are a child of the devil and an enemy of everything that is right.'" (verse 9-10a)

Far from being a "Son of the Saviour", this man was a child of the devil, and God makes it clear to Saul what is going on. Not only does he have the spiritual discernment to recognise a man who is *"full of all kinds of deceit and* trickery", who *"never stops perverting the right way for the Lord"*, but he is moved to confront this spiritual opposition in the name of God. *"Now the hand of the Lord is against you. You are going to be blind, and for a time you will not even able to see the light of the sun"* (verse 11).

We should note that there is no dialogue with evil; this is simply a command that the man of God gives in the name of God. Saul recognises Satan's intimidation and takes up his authority. Perhaps he saw an echo of his own earlier disobedience as an opponent of the gospel and the persecutor of Christians. Just as he had been humbled and blinded for a time during his own conversion experience, so he declares the same judgement over Elymas.

The results of Saul taking up his authority are significant.

"Immediately mist and darkness came over him (Elymas) and he groped around seeking someone to lead him by the hand. When the proconsul saw what had happened, he believed, for he was amazed at the teaching about the Lord." (verses 11b-12)

Elymas' lies were exposed and God's power is shown to be greater than that of the enemy. Sergius Paulus believes because he saw, but he was amazed at the teaching he heard. Just as in the ministry of Jesus, the word and the works go together to bring people to faith. But what really intrigues me is the change in Saul; henceforth he is always known as "Paul", and he is always named first. He becomes the person God created him to be.

We can't simply speak out and expect that things will always happen. Authority has to be based on a firm understanding of who we are. There's a comical example of this later in Acts with the seven sons of Sceva (Acts 19:14f). These Jewish exorcists have discovered the power of the name of Jesus, but don't have the authority to use it because they have no relationship with him and no firm foundation of identity as sons of God. But when we know who we are, something wonderful becomes possible.

Knowing our identity leads to authority. Picking up that authority and using it releases us into our destiny. By destiny, I don't mean necessarily a specific or mystical plan for your life, but rather the point of your existence. We are placed in this world to advance the Kingdom of God and to confront the kingdom of Satan in whatever sphere God gives us.

There is no part of life, no square metre of ground, no stream of culture that God doesn't claim as his own – and he wants to use us to help take it back. Usually where God has placed you in life is precisely where he wants to use you. The nature of salvation is not simply being saved *from* something, but is also being saved *for* something. It's finding a new purpose in becoming God's soldiers and servants in our families, communities, institutions and workplaces.

Recognising that battle, and taking up our authority within it, changes the way that we pray and the way that we minister. Few prayers offered in our churches sound much like the prayers in the Bible. As Walter Wink put it, "The fawning etiquette of unctuous prayer is utterly foreign to the Bible. Biblical prayer is impertinent, persistent, shameless, indecorous ... It is more like haggling in an oriental bazaar than the polite monologues of the churches."[1] Our Bible translations don't always help either. The heart of the Lord's Prayer, for example, is *"Your Kingdom come, your will be done."* That could sound like a polite or even wistful longing, but the Greek words have the force of a command: *"Kingdom of God, come; Will of God, be done!"* In praying for the sick, or in breaking the hold of evil, learning to use our authority as believers enables us to see the Kingdom break through far more frequently.

It is often noted that Jesus' final (private) instructions to his disciples before the cross, as recorded for us in John's gospel, centre on the work of the Holy Spirit. In the other gospels, however, we have recorded his final *public* teaching before the cross. Matthew, Mark and Luke all include Jesus' description of signs at the end of the age, but only Matthew adds three parables that speak about the disciples' tasks until his return.[2] In Matthew 25 we read that, in the light of Jesus' Second Coming, his disciples are to be ready (verses 1-13), be responsible (verses 14-30), and be righteous (verses 31-46). That central parable, the Parable of the Talents, explains "being responsible" as being like stewards who have been given oversight of the Master's resources. Different servants receive different amounts, but all are expected to make use of what they were given. Those who put their entrustment to work discover that they can multiply it and, in return, are entrusted with more – and with it the invitation to *"come and share in your Master's happiness"* (verses 21, 23).

The harsh words are reserved for the servant who does nothing with what he's been given, and even goes as far as to say that he fears the Master's response to any possible failure. The result of that refusal to put into practice what he has been given, and the slander on the character of the Master that it implies, is that he is judged in line with his jaundiced view of his Master.

This is a forceful way of Jesus saying that he expects us to take up and use what we have been given – and that our refusal to do so reveals that we still think of God as a demanding judge and fear his punishment. By this time, he clearly expected his disciples to know the love that cast out that fear (as we saw from 1 John 4:18). To redeem some secular lyrics from an old song, you do have to "use it before you lose it!"

The argument of this book is that we'll come to these places many times as we grow spiritually. We might learn to take up our authority in one aspect of life and ministry, but have many others where we are yet to feel confident. I went to theological college having only ever preached once in public. Over time, I've grown comfortable in that gift. I even feel that I understand 1 Peter 4:11 (*"If anyone speaks, he should do it as one speaking the very words of God"*). I've grown to be confident that, as I do my best to preach, weak and imperfect though I am, God will be speaking through me. I don't need to apologise or underplay the gift of God. Obviously, I'm not claiming to be the greatest preacher in the world, but I'm confident that it is a gift in my life that God uses and so it carries a measure of authority. In other areas, I haven't picked up the authority as I might.

One such area, until recent years, was in deliverance. I'd often been involved in times of prayer when I sensed that some level of demonic oppression was being broken from someone's life, but I had few stories of dramatic confrontations with deep-rooted evil. I rationalised that this was something God was more likely to use my friends in performing. We all have our specialities, don't we? I was quite happy to leave that aspect of ministry to others, even though I believed in it.

However, I started to feel that I was denying something that was clear in the Bible. When teaching on Jesus' call of the disciples in Mark 3, as we saw in chapter 2, I noticed that he didn't actually mention healing! This was problematic – I was using the verse to justify our call to share in Jesus' ministry of signs and wonders, which I am convinced is right, but actually the only two activities mentioned are preaching and casting out demons.

"Jesus went up on a mountain side and called to him those he wanted and they came to him. He appointed twelve that they might be with him and that he might send them out to preach and have authority to drive out demons." (Mark 3:13-15)

Clearly this aspect of the in-breaking of the Kingdom was more central than I had acknowledged, and not just for the few but for all disciples.[3] But I wasn't confident that I had much authority in this area. That gradually began to change as I learnt more of the principles in this book, about my identity and the authority that came with it, and as I started to step out and exercise that authority. I came to a much clearer understanding of what the Scriptures teach in this area. It was an enormous help to be around Robby Dawkins in several times of ministry and to receive his encouragement for what he saw me doing. (Robby used to play American Football. Until recently I think I rather assumed that it was his physical size that scared demons into fleeing...).

If there was a particular breakthrough, it came when I was leading a retreat for New Wine in Sweden. We were gathered up in the mountains in a log cabin in beautiful scenery, alongside a frozen lake and amongst the pine trees. On arrival, we had seen an elk running along the edge of the ice. It was idyllic, but there wasn't anywhere else to go – and I was due to be the sole teacher for 25 church leaders for an entire week. That's a lot of teaching sessions, but the ones that I was least confident about were those where I was meant to teach about deliverance ministry. In my church, we have a good practice and quite a lot of experience in that area but, as I said, I tended to leave the ministry to those who felt called to it.

At the end of that session though, one leader asked

whether I thought there might be a specific demonic attack on her son. He had always been the one to whom everything bad would happen. If they were going on holiday, the family joke was that he would break some bone shortly before they left. On a number of occasions, illness or accidents had seriously affected his life.

I felt immediately that this wasn't normal so replied that it was certainly worth praying into! In the time of ministry, without expecting it, as I prayed for her I felt a great anger rise up from inside me and found myself rebuking the spirit of death that was coming against her and her family, whereupon she fell to the floor. Later, the other pastors told me that this was extremely out of character for her. At the same time as she fell, one of the pastors in a group across the room turned round and said, ashen-faced, "What was that? Something flew past my leg!"

Trying to be matter of fact, I said, "Don't worry, let's just pray that nothing can attach to you" and asked people to pray prayers of protection and cleansing over him. (I suppose, if I'd known more about what I was doing, and remembered the relevant Bible passage, I could have tried to send the spirit into the elk ... not fair to such a magnificent creature though).

I'm still not attracted to the idea of deliverance ministry. Few people are! But I know that since then I'm much more confident that, should the need arise, I have the authority and I know how to use it. I think I took another step that day into becoming the Paul that God wants me to be.

Notes

1. Walter Wink, as quoted in John Ortberg, *The Life You've Always Wanted*, Zondervan, 1997.

2. Luke has his own version of the Parable of the Talents, usually referred to as the Parable of the Pounds/Ten Minas, but locates it a week or so earlier in Jesus' ministry (Luke 19:12-27).

3. There is further training on healing and deliverance in the New Wine resource series, *Learning to Heal* (book, DVD and study guide for small groups). Given the sensitive pastoral implications around this subject, every church and denomination has guidelines for how this ministry should be carried out. It is important that you operate within them for your own protection and that of others.

7
Destiny leads to obedience

"Once upon a time in Springfield, the Simpson family visited a new supermarket. Monstromart's slogan was 'where shopping is a baffling ordeal'. Product choice was unlimited, shelving reached the ceiling, nutmeg came in 12lb boxes and the express checkout had a sign reading, '1,000 items or less'. In the end the Simpsons returned to Apu's Kwik-E-Mart." (Stuart Jeffries, writing in The Guardian, 21/10/15)

Too much choice is stressing us out. In 2015, Tesco decided to scrap 30,000 of the 90,000 products that they were offering in their supermarkets. This was in response to the success of other retailers like Aldi and Lidl, which offer "only" between 2000 and 3000 different products.

Times have changed. Only a generation or two ago, customers shopping for shampoo would face a few simple choices. Modern shampoo was introduced in the 1930s, but now is available in a bewildering variety of options. You can have shampoo for extra shine, bounce, strength, colour; shampoos that reduce dandruff or that are anti-bacterial; shampoos that aid the re-growth of hair; or shampoos with almost any extra ingredient that you could imagine – almost any herb you could name, fruit, vegetables, honey, proteins, even beers...

What's driving this explosion of different products, many from the same companies? Simply this: we live in a consumer age. Consumerism places us at the centre of the world. It appeals to our ego by telling us that we have the power to choose because we are special. There might be only tiny differences between many of the things on sale, but that doesn't matter – "the customer is king"! Major advertising campaigns play on our vanity. One fast food chain tells us that, "you can have it your way"; a shampoo is sold with the strapline "because you're worth it". It seems that this is an effective way to sell products.

Of course, the Church isn't immune. We are surrounded by consumerism and bombarded with messages that reinforce its worldview. So consumerism can easily bleed into the way that we view our faith. Most of us have chosen the church that we regularly attend because it suits our needs and our preferred spiritual path to encountering God. That's probably okay – no one church can express the variety of Christian worship, suit every personality, or be effective in reaching all sections of society equally well. However, all too easily we are seduced into thinking that the church we attend is ultimately there to meet our needs. We want things the way that we like them, and we make our feelings known when we don't get our way. We can fall into the trap of attending services for "what we can get out of them", rather than "what we can bring to God as an offering". We ought to gather to encourage each other and to seek God, so that we can then love and serve him better, but consumerism promotes selfishness. It may be an effective way to increase companies' profits, but its a terrible way to be a disciple. The customer is NOT king, Jesus is!

Thinking like a consumer will prevent you from growing as a disciple. There seems to be a slippery slope involved. We start out as "consumers" – always evaluating things by what we can get rather than what we can give. This leads to us becoming "connoisseurs" – people who know how to taste the offering, and who know what they do and don't like. Inevitably that will lead us to act as "critics" – making judgements on whatever is on offer, such as the worship leader's capabilities, or the speaker's gifts.

Preferences can easily become judgments. Sadly, the end result of this is that we slide into being "cynics" – unable to receive what God is doing or saying through the person, because we've already judged the packaging. We forget that, when God uses someone, he can only ever work through broken and weak people. In fact, the Bible seems to suggest that those who appear to have it all together are the least likely to be truly used by him.

We break out of this mindset by coming back to the heart of discipleship – hearing the call of Jesus and responding to him. Jesus was not interested in putting on a show, nor is there a version of discipleship which puts us at the centre. His message was not one of self-fulfilment, self-actualisation or even self-improvement. Instead, he calls us to lay down our own lives in order that we might be reborn and find our true nature as we follow him.

There is a passage in John's gospel that I think speaks into this modern-day challenge. In John 12, just after Jesus has ridden into Jerusalem on a donkey, being triumphantly acclaimed by the crowds, some Greeks approach Philip with the request, *"Sir, we would like to see Jesus"* (John 12:21). You would think that this would be an excellent opportunity for Jesus to further build the momentum for change that the Triumphal Entry had shown – people, including those from far afield, wanted to hear what he had to say.

Jesus' response, however, turns our expectations on their head. *"The hour has come for the Son of Man to be glorified. I tell you the truth, unless a grain of wheat falls to the ground and dies, it remains only a single seed. But if it dies, it produces many seeds"* (verses 23-24a). Far from welcoming the attention, Jesus seems to be trying to put the Greeks off by talking about dying! Obviously what Jesus has in mind is his own death, the "hour" for which is now close at hand. It seems that Jesus isn't interested in building the crowds

– what he seeks are converts. People who will let him be Master and who willingly take the role of disciples.

As we've seen already, disciples do what Jesus did. We are trained to do the same works and speak the same message that he did. We live his risen life and share in the same Spirit. In a sense, that is what Jesus is actually speaking about here. *"Unless a grain of wheat falls to the ground and dies, it remains a single seed. But if it dies, it produces many seeds"* (verse 24). Most often in the gospels, Jesus speaks of his death as a saving work. Here he speaks of it as something that multiplies life. His death on the cross is the death that *"produces many seeds"*, many of the same type of life, even many lives that have the same multiplicative power within them. The answer to the problem of Jesus not being able to meet the needs of the crowds whilst in his earthly ministry – *"the harvest is plentiful but the workers are few"* – was to send the disciples out with power and authority (Matthew 9:35-10:1). The ultimate aim was for all his disciples, in every age, to share his life and carry that same power and authority.

But disciples aren't formed from crowds. You cannot call someone "Master" when your own needs and comforts are uppermost on your agenda. The Greeks were confronted with that very same challenge. *"The man who loves his life will lose it, while the man who hates his life in this world will keep it for eternal life"* (John 12:25).

Using typically black and white language to make the point, Jesus calls them (and us) to make the only choice that matters – who gets to be in charge, Jesus or ourselves? "Loving your life" in this world means "holding onto the things this world can offer as being of greatest value"; "hating your life" in this world simply means comprehensively rejecting that attitude. It doesn't mean being unable to enjoy life. After all, Jesus was full of joy in the people that he met and in the things that he did, but only because he was living for the Kingdom that was coming.

He wants us to share the same joy, but it won't be found in living for our own little empires. The demand he makes is total, but only because he loves us and wants the best for us.

The next verse bears close inspection, because it contains a principle of being a disciple which, in my experience, we often neglect.

"Whoever serves me must follow me; and where I am, my servant also will be. My Father will honour the one who serves me." (John 12:26)

It occurred to me some years ago that this verse is the opposite of what we might expect. I think we would anticipate that Jesus would say that, if we want to follow him, we must become servants. That would make sense – surely being a disciple is about what we do with our lives? But instead Jesus puts it the other way round – if we want to serve him, then we must follow him.

Putting it that way, he makes it impossible for us to think of discipleship as "good works". It isn't about what we do; its about whether we do what HE asks us to do. Discipleship then cannot be separated from an intimate relationship with Jesus. It requires us to learn to hear his voice and to develop hearts that are quick to obey what he asks of us. It requires that we see where he is at work and join him. That is the path to true discipleship and the way to be honoured in heaven.

In the previous chapter we looked at how we can only step into God's plan for our lives, our "destiny", if we take up the authority that we have been given and see ourselves on a mission. But our mission is not to go charging off on our own. At the end of Matthew's gospel, Jesus promised that when he sends us, he will go with us (Matthew 28:20). Fulfilling whatever calling we are given comes from learning to hear his voice and obey. He's already at work, and his ways are always better than ours. I've lost count of the number of times, as a church leader, that we've tried to do something but found ourselves frustrated until we prayed into it. Having prayed, a new idea came and with that came a breakthrough! I think we would all make faster progress if we prioritised listening to Jesus' voice and sought to follow rather than lead.

The desire to find our destiny is deep within us all. We demand that our lives have meaning and purpose, because we know instinctively that our lives are meant to count for something. We want to have a cause, something for which to live. We mustn't allow that thought to paralyse us though. It's all too easy for Christians to become overly-introspective. We can be so worried about what God wants us to do with our lives that we stop doing the very things that would help us discover it. Destiny doesn't come to us fully formed or totally clarified. Even Paul took many years to begin to understand the fullness of the words that he heard in his conversion encounter with the risen Lord.

My advice would be, "just do something!" Frequently, I've suggested that people simply start obeying what they hear Jesus saying when they are reading their Bibles alone, or when his Spirit whispers to them to cross the room and start a conversation. Start trying to develop the habit of instantaneous obedience and you'll start stepping into greater clarity. After all, a moving object is easier for God to steer ... and harder for Satan to hit!

It's when we have a sense of where and how God wants to use us, even if it's simply starting where we are, that we can learn to walk closely with Jesus. That's when we experience true satisfaction in life. When the disciples left Jesus at the well in Samaria to go off shopping for food, they had no idea that this would be life-changing for a desperately sad woman and, in time, for her whole community (John 4). As the Samaritan woman approached, coming to draw water at a time of day when no one else would, because of her shameful history of relationships, I believe that Jesus and the Father were speaking to each other.

Having had his attention drawn to her, Jesus uses divine wisdom (to bring the conversation around to her deepest needs) and supernatural revelation (*"you have had five husbands...")* to convince her of his relationship with God. When the disciples returned, they didn't know what to make of the fact that he was talking to a woman and simply came back to the issue of his need for physical nourishment. *"But he said to them, 'I have food to eat that you know nothing about'"* (verse 32). As was so often the case, the disciples missed the point and wondered who had come out from the town to feed him.

"'My food,' said Jesus, 'is to do the will of him who sent me and to finish his work.'" (verse 34)

There is no feeling as great as knowing that you are doing what the Father wants you to do. I heard someone once describe it as "knowing the Father's smile on your life". For me, that confirms my sense of vocation. There are times when I'm preaching, or when I'm bringing some leadership to bear on the future of our church, when I feel God's smile. Don't imagine that this is a constant experience, but it is frequent enough that I know what it means. It helps me be confident that I'm doing what God has called me to do, that I'm using the gifts that he has given me in the right way, and that I'm being the person that he called me to be. I believe that is an experience he wants us all to enjoy. It's like spiritual gifts though – you don't know what your gifts are until you try to do things. And you won't know your unique contribution in the Kingdom until you step out in obedience to what you hear.

It is a principle in the Kingdom that we start where we are, but we grow as we use what we have. Gideon, the frightened young man dubbed "Mighty Warrior" by the Angel of the Lord, was told, *"Go in the strength you have"* (Judges 6:14). Jesus said, *"whoever can be trusted with very little can also be trusted with much"* (Luke 16:10). He also said, *"To everyone who has, more will be given"* (Luke 19:26). John Wimber would often say, especially with regard to learning to heal, "If you want more, give away what you've got." In other words, the path to growth is putting into practice what we have learnt and understood. Likewise, the path to realising our destiny is being obedient in the little things, and taking the first steps into whatever God has shown us.

Obeying doesn't mean always succeeding though. When you learnt to ride a bicycle, I doubt very much that you succeeded on your first try. There would have been wobbles, even outright crashes. It might well have felt very unnatural to you. Those early experiences shouldn't have caused you to conclude that you were unable or unsuited to ride a bike. You just needed more practice. In fact, you probably had help. Many of us learnt to ride by having our father run alongside us. The reality, in all likelihood, was that we were hardly cycling at all. I'm sure many of us gained the confidence that we were cycling when actually our father was holding the bike upright and pushing us along! In time, though, he gave us less support until we were moving freely on our own. Although he never leaves us on our own, I think our heavenly Father gives us additional support as we take our first faltering steps into new things.

Some years ago, I had an object lesson on this myself. Life can be very demanding, so I had been reading a book about leading a church in a healthy way and avoiding burnout. Actually, it would be more truthful to say that I had been meaning to read it, but I hadn't gotten around to it! Fortunately, I have a loving wife who has a vested interest in keeping me alive and well. She took the book from my desk, read it, underlined the actions it suggested that I needed to take and returned it to me with a checklist.

Top of the list was the need to take regular thinking days, retreats and times of solitude. By personality, I am an extrovert and an activist, so nothing could sound worse to my ears. Nevertheless, I placed some dates in my diary. When one came round, I realised the day before that I hadn't made any arrangements to go away. As a result, I must be the only person ever who has taken a quiet retreat in the food court of Westfield Shopping City, Stratford! It suited my personality perfectly though. I parked myself with a stack of books on healing, a pancake breakfast meal, some coffee and had a thoroughly wonderful time.

After several hours I was full of faith for physical healing. Not by nature an evangelist, I had been feeling a passion to be used by God more in my everyday life. I'd been praying for healing in church settings for years, often with non-Christians, but hungered to see more in spontaneous encounters outside of the church walls. So,

I packed my books away and resolved that I would be available and responsive to any opportunity that the Lord showed me. Before leaving the shopping centre for home, I went to visit the toilets. As in many shopping centres, these were located down a long corridor and, as I entered, I was confronted with a crowd of people coming towards – seemingly all on crutches, walking with sticks or being pushed in wheelchairs! I can only think that the local Stroke Club were having an outing. To be honest, it was completely overwhelming and I simply walked past.

I did feel bad though, and resolved to look for someone with whom I could pray on the way out. Coming back into the corridor, I saw an elderly black lady walking towards me with a stick and immediately felt, "she's the one". However, before she reached me, she turned into the disabled toilets that were nearer the entrance. I walked back out to the food court and was ready to give up and go home when I thought, "I did set this day aside in my diary, so I don't have anything better to do. Perhaps I ought to wait for her."

I hadn't quite thought through what that might look like, but fortunately there were other people waiting in the corridor for friends and loved ones, so I wasn't alone. She was some time in coming out – to be honest, I was starting to wonder if she'd passed out in there – but I held on and eventually she emerged. Trying my best to look approachable and non-threatening, I smiled as she limped past, caught her eye and said, "That looks painful, are you alright?"

Somewhat taken aback, the lady did at least reply, "Thank you. It is. I had a hip operation some months ago and I've been in constant pain every since." Sensing my chance, I said, "Well, I'm a Christian and I've been learning more about how to pray for healing. I've seen people healed before in Jesus' name. Would you allow me to pray for you now?"

She replied, "No thanks, I'm a Jehovah's Witness"... and hobbled away!

All I could do was leave (which involved overtaking her again – she wasn't fast) and swallow my pride. As I came out of the corridor, I was going over the whole encounter in my mind and wondering, "What was the point of that then?" It was then that I felt the Lord say to me, "It'll be a lot easier next time..."

The truth is that it has been. By surviving that awkward incident with only bruising to my ego, I've been much more able to take risks. I've prayed for people in many everyday settings since, and often seen God touch them with his power. Conversations about God have followed on every occasion. And I've not regretted taking those risks. What is the worst that could happen? Once you realise that apparent failure might make you look foolish, but doesn't reflect badly on God, you don't have much to lose. After all, if our self-worth comes from the knowledge of his love and affirmation, and from our identity as sons and daughters, then stepping out in faith is only going to bring joy to our Father.

Obeying doesn't always mean succeeding. Often it looks

like trying, failing, learning and thereby growing, so that we can try again, but perhaps be better next time. That's how we grow into all that God has for us.

8
Obedience leads to intimacy

The truth doesn't set you free.

I wish it did. All we would need to do would be to broadcast it, or simply go door to door telling people the truth, and then everyone would be free. We wouldn't see anyone struggling with addictions anymore, or bound up by the deceptions and false values that the media often peddles. Yet, of course, Jesus did say, *"The truth will set you free"* (John 8:32).

What we must always do when reading our Bibles, is check the context rather than simply take a verse (or, in this case, part of a verse) and read it in isolation. That verse actually says, *"Then you will know the truth, and the truth will set you free."* The truth must be *known* before it helps us. But there's also a condition added in order for us to receive that knowledge: "THEN you will know the truth". We need to look at the preceding verse as well, so that the whole passage reads: *"To the Jews who had believed him, Jesus said, 'If you hold to my teaching, you are really my disciples. Then you will know the truth, and the truth will set you free"* (John 8:31-32).

The freedom that Jesus brings cannot be separated from being in a relationship with him. Faith is required – they had believed him: following him is essential – then they would really become his disciples. What that looked like would be obedience – *"hold to my teaching..."*. Again, there is no sense here that all you need to do is adopt certain behaviours, because the right actions cannot be separated from having a relationship with Jesus.

However, if you want to go deeper in that relationship and experience the freedom that Jesus offers, then you need to learn how to obey him because the fruit of obedience is revelation and freedom. The "truth that sets you free" is the one that you discover in an intimate relationship with Jesus, and that intimacy comes from holding to his teaching. Jesus *is* the Truth.

That's the surprising thing about obedience. It sounds like duty, but it's actually joy. Obedience leads to a closer intimacy with God. In John 8, the dialogue between Jesus and some of those present moves straight into a discussion on the theme of being children of God. Without taking on that identity as sons and daughters, even trying to do the right thing can end up leading us away from God rather than to him. Obedience doesn't establish a standing with

God, because it is grace alone that brings us into God's family. Once in the family though, obedience is how we demonstrate our love for God – and it always brings us deeper into the experience of that intimate love.

"Obedience" gets a bad press in today's world. We live in an "anti-authority" age. Many institutions have been discredited, often because they have abused their authority and demanded unquestioning obedience. In the Church there has been a reaction against the harsh preaching of some teachers in previous generations, which left listeners with a view of God as a cruel and demanding Judge, who was waiting for us to step out of line so that he could punish us. Rediscovering grace has been vital for the renewal of the faith in our generation, yet it has led to two popular misconceptions.

One is that obedience is only part of the Law, and therefore not something we need. "God loves you just as you are. You don't need to get cleaned up in order to come to God. You are accepted, therefore you don't need to change your behaviour in order to be a Christian." Building on wonderful truths, but airbrushing out other things that Jesus says, leads to a weak and ineffective message. Repentance and transformation are part of the gospel.

The second misconception is that obedience could never be something that would be attractive to us. How we understand obedience makes a huge difference to whether or not we'll embrace it!

Obedience is not sacrifice. In the Old Testament, when God's people were learning to walk with him, he gave them a sacrificial code so that they would learn more about him and have a means of showing their faithfulness. The problem with religion though, is that the outward forms have a tendency to take over from the inner truths they are meant to express. The prophets were constantly having to call the people back to the heart of worship:

"For when I brought your ancestors out of Egypt and spoke to them, I did not just give them commands about burnt offerings and sacrifices, but I gave them this command: Obey me, and I will be your God and you will be my people. Walk in obedience to all I command you, that it may go well with you." (Jeremiah 7:22-23)

In other words, obeying God is about living in his family, as his children. And obeying God is the pathway to blessing.

The thing to remember is that God is good. He is the perfect, loving Heavenly Father. That means that his commandments are not arbitrary or negative. He only commands what he knows would be for our best. Many people will be familiar with this old sermon illustration: a child might not understand why he isn't allowed to play with the block of sharp kitchen knives, but that doesn't mean that the parent is bad or a kill-joy for setting that rule. Quite the opposite! The same is true with parents trying to reinforce a reasonable bedtime, responsible use of the Internet, or a balanced and healthy diet. The commandment comes from love. Being obedient is therefore also about love. We show that we believe that God is good, and that he has our best in mind, by doing what he asks, even when sometimes we don't feel like it. Obedience is like a love-gift back to God.

The link between love and obedience is one of the characteristic themes of the gospel and epistles written by *"the disciple whom Jesus loved"*, John. In John 14:23, Jesus says, *"Anyone who loves me will obey my teaching. My Father will love them, and we will come to them and make our home with them."* That highlights God's part – how obedience leads us into a greater experience of intimacy with him. In 1 John 2:3-5, we read, *"We know that we have come to know him if we keep his commands ... if anyone obeys his word, love for God is truly made complete in them."* The emphasis there is on our part in expressing love for him in return, but even then we receive blessing – we have the confident assurance of our relationship with him. We know that we're God's children because he's loved us, and because we love him!

In some ways, "obedience-intimacy" is a little circle within our larger circle of spiritual growth. It's like a summary of all that we've looked at so far. Throughout the gospels, Jesus offers us several of these summaries, each opening up a different angle on what it is to be in relationship with God. What should we do when we hear the gospel? We should *"repent and believe the good news"* (Mark 1:15). What shows that we are Jesus' disciples?

Pruning and fruitfulness (John 15:2). What is the heart of discipleship? Obedience and intimacy.

You could even say that obedience is our gift to ourselves. Choosing to obey God is always choosing the better thing. By contrast, I think we've often associated obedience with self-restraint. For some of us, this is almost hard-wired into our personalities. As an oldest child, I've always been interested in the long-held theory that the order in which you and your siblings are born has an impact on your personality as an adult. While it may not hold up for every person ever born, studies indicate that there is a great deal of truth in this theory. It is surely significant, for example, that 100% of astronauts who have gone into space were either eldest children or, at least, eldest sons with older sisters. (First-borns are the greatest!) First-born traits include being conscientious, reliable and responsible (though we can also be overly cautious, even controlling – as well as more prone to divorce than middle children, less socially skilled than the youngest children, etc). Each birth order type has its strengths and weaknesses, but some of us are more prone to seeing everything in terms of "duty" – the "should" and "ought" approach to life.

I wonder whether that's why some of us struggle to change. We may be trying to confront our issues, whether patterns of sin, habits or addictions, by using willpower alone. Intellectually, we may understand grace but practically we rarely allow ourselves to experience it. That can lead to a Christianity where we work hard to try and improve, but end up settling for maintaining a good front, a public image of holiness, with a deep sense of frustration and shame over the inner reality of our lives. We have to come to the realisation that we can't achieve holiness on our own. True transformation takes the deep work of the Spirit, whereas we were relying on willpower and making it all about us.

One way of diagnosing whether that is an issue in your own discipleship is asking yourself whether you think of obedience largely in terms of holding yourself back from something that you want to do. Thinking like that is to miss the point. In a famous sermon in the early 19th century, a Scottish preacher called Thomas Chalmers made the point that if we tell someone to stop sinning then at best they may achieve it only reluctantly and partially. If we give them a vision of knowing God and his glory then they will gladly root out all that gets in the way of a relationship with God.

He entitled his sermon "The Expulsive Power of a New Affection". Becoming people who love God more than any substitute is the way to break the power of the flesh. Or as the prophet Jonah put it from the belly of the whale, *"Those who cling to worthless idols turn away from God's love for them"* (Jonah 2:8). Obedience comes most easily and naturally from desiring God more than anything else.

The most powerful illustration I ever had of that truth came when we had a dog. Becky and I have two wonderful children, Joshua and Rachel. Joshua is now in his late teens but is autistic and has never really learnt to speak. Although he is man-sized, in many ways his behaviours are like that of a toddler or a pre-school age child. This makes life quite demanding at home and so those who care for us, friends and members of the congregation, will often pass on stories about therapies, treatments, diets or teaching techniques that have helped other children with autism. In 2006, a drama was broadcast on television called "After Thomas". Loosely based on a true story, it was about a boy with autism and how his relationship with a golden retriever puppy helped him to break out of his isolated world, developing empathy and social skills. So many people mentioned the film to us that, eventually, we caved. We got a dog.

Unfortunately, we got an autistic dog.

At least, it felt like that! Fergus was a golden retriever, the runt of the litter, chosen with great care by the breeder for his docile nature and high pain threshold. To test this, the dog breeders will usually squeeze a toe until the dog reacts. On reflection, Fergus' "high pain threshold" was probably more a sign of his being as dumb as a rock. If you've read the book *Marley and Me: Life and Love with the World's Worst Dog*[1], or seen the film, you will know how much work a large dog can be. Joshua and Fergus formed something of a symbiotic relationship, with Joshua gaining a large animal to use as a pillow and Fergus gaining a near-constant source of food falling to the floor, but I'm not sure it helped Joshua in the ways that we had hoped. Nevertheless, Fergus was a sweet natured dog and, overall, a positive addition to the household. Our main problems with him were around walks.

From the beginning, Fergus was madly enthusiastic about getting out of the house. For him, the outside world was something he couldn't wait to explore, and your pace was never fast enough to get there. Fergus also never saw a dog or a person that he didn't want to meet. The end result of this boundless energy, coupled with sheer strength, meant that walking Fergus was somewhat akin to water skiing.

On several occasions, Fergus took off to see someone or something, pulling Becky off her feet and onto the ground, or wrenching her shoulder. A regular collar was replaced with a choke chain, but all that happened was that we now had an enthusiastic dog who was making a good attempt at self-strangulation. Walks weren't pretty. More experienced dog owners – which in this case means "anyone who has ever had a dog" – would often comment that something was off in our dog-walking technique. Eventually we gave in and admitted that we needed help.

We turned up at the remedial dog-training centre with little hope and a lot of shame. The instructors asked us to show them how we would walk Fergus around the paddock. Being animal lovers, I think they only let us get about half way round before they stepped in and said, "No, no, that's not right!" Rather than the lead being tight enough to play a tune upon, apparently it was meant to make a nice, loose parabolic curve from the owner's hand to the dog's collar. Who knew? They instructed us to leave him with them for a couple of hours and then return.

When we came back, there was Fergus trotting along next to the instructor, with no choking sounds and in the correct position, head close and slightly behind the walker. You can imagine how stunned we were. How had this magic been achieved? When I asked the trainers, they replied, "Simple. You have a little pouch on your belt, filled with pieces of liver and you keep slipping the dog titbits as you walk." The idea was that the dog, wanting to get the treats, would come to associate being next to the human's hip with being fed. And it worked! Rather than charging on to the next person or dog, Fergus was learning that where he really wanted to be was alongside his walker, with his head at the walker's hip, because that's where the good stuff was.

We never completely mastered the art of dog walking, but it improved significantly. More importantly, I learnt something about obedience. Obedience leads to intimacy. The idea that obedience is essentially about self-restraint, pulling forward towards sin, but holding yourself at the end of the lead (and often choking yourself), just isn't accurate. It's actually about wanting to stay close to God because you know where it is that you'll be satisfied. Anything that might separate you or create distance in your relationship loses much of its appeal, because all you really want is him.

The New Testament says in a couple of places that Jesus *"learned obedience"*[2]. Yet he never sinned, which means that he wasn't ever disobedient! Learning obedience therefore must be much more than simply not doing what is wrong – it actually comes down to learning how to love God and draw ever closer to him. If that was the case for our Master, it will be so for us. Our spiritual growth will always centre on developing deeper intimacy with our Father.

Notes

1. *Marley and Me: Life and Love with the World's Worst Dog*, John Grogan, Hodder and Stoughton, 2005.
2. Luke 2:51 (to his parents), Hebrew 5:8 (through what he suffered).

9
Spiralling upwards

In earlier chapters, I mentioned that Becky was from America, so many of our holidays have been to fly back to see family and friends in St Louis. In the last chapter, however, I also spoke a little about Joshua being autistic. Any parent who has ever flown with children will know how stressful an experience it can be, and it's doubly so when you're travelling with a child with special needs. When Joshua was small, we managed, but, as he grew, long-haul transatlantic flights became an increasingly challenging proposition.

Almost everything about flying was hard for him – queueing to check in, carrying bags through the concourse to the gate, having to sit in a seat and remain strapped in for hours... The stewards and stewardesses were usually very kind and understanding, especially when he was younger and cuter, but they didn't like him crawling under the seats rather than having his seatbelt fastened. They didn't like him running up and down the aisles. And they certainly didn't like him trying to open the door at 35,000 feet! Ten hours of that is a long time. And when you landed at the other end, there would be more waiting and queuing... Becky would be stressed for months before we flew, dreading how it might turn out.

The first thing we tried was medication. The doctor kindly prescribed Temazepam, a form of Valium. That really helped Becky, but I'm not sure it made any difference to Joshua! (That was a joke – but it truly didn't seem to work for Joshua). We were just on the verge of giving up on the idea of flying when a friend suggested that we get wheelchair assistance. You have to understand that this had never occurred to us because Joshua has no mobility issues, on the contrary he's much more likely to run away from us. However, our friend Gill, who is a nurse, knew that it would be relatively easy to arrange with the doctor's support and thought it would be a great help.

It was fantastic. We had an extra adult to help carry bags. We were moved to the front of every queue, whether check-in or passport control. We were driven to the gate in a buggy and seated first on the plane. And on arrival we were met with someone else to give us the same help all over again. Joshua loved sitting in the wheelchair and being pushed through the airport.

The only problem was the looks we received when he jumped out of the chair and ran down the corridor.

I don't know what you'd do in that situation as a parent? When everyone is looking at you, thinking that you'd fraudulently acquired special treatment? I decided that all I could do was draw on my faith.

"Hallelujah! It's a miracle!"

I'm not sure that anyone was fooled. But it did make me think. Why not? Shouldn't we be hopeful and expectant of more people springing from their wheelchairs, physically restored and *"walking and jumping, and praising God"*?[1] And though Joshua has been well prayed for over the years, why shouldn't the next prayer be the one that makes the great difference?

I think that anyone who follows Jesus and hears about miracles wants to experience them. For some though, their theological framework may tell them that those days are over. Others may not want to believe because they've experienced disappointment when they've prayed before and don't want to expose themselves to further pain. Most perhaps believe, but don't expect. "These things happen through others and I praise God for them, but they don't happen through me," runs the thought.

"We settle for mediocrity, because it's believable and achievable, and because we think it's what we deserve," as Steven Furtick said recently[2].

This book has been an attempt to suggest some pathways to a greater and more consistent experience of Kingdom ministry – the things that Jesus sent his first disciples to do, and which remain part of our calling today. Miracles of healing and deliverance can happen as soon as we believe and make ourselves available to God. All that is required is trust. But they can happen more frequently as we grow in faith and take more risks. There's always more than we have yet experienced, and God longs for us to enter into that "more".

It might have surprised you that, in a book on spiritual growth, there hasn't been a greater emphasis on the traditional Christian disciplines up to this point. That's because the aim of those practices is always to lead us into encounter with God so that we are changed, and this book has focussed on how we will be changed by those experiences. Jesus criticised the Pharisees for allowing the outward form to become a substitute for the inward substance: *"You study the scriptures diligently because you think that in them you have eternal life. These are the very scriptures that testify about me, yet you refuse to come to me to have life"* (John 5:39-40).

There's no doubt that we should all prioritise spending time in personal prayer, in reading and reflecting on God's Word, and in enjoying his presence in corporate worship. We should hunger and thirst after God. We should embrace self-denial in order to seek the things of the Kingdom. Do these things and you will tend to grow – if you remember that we do them in order to meet with Jesus. What we are seeking from our spiritual disciplines is not information and reassurance, but revelation and life-changing encounter.

The fruits of those practices will be lives built on deep foundations of confidence in who we are in God and what he wants to do through us. Spiritual growth will look like an ever-deepening grasp of the things that we've been looking at in this little book. And the deeper the foundation, the more that can be built upon it.

That's why "growing in circles" is really a half-truth – in reality, we are spiralling upwards. In our journey into discipleship, we come back to confront the same truths again and again, but each time hopefully a little more profoundly. The *"upward call of God in Christ Jesus"*, as some translations of Philippians 3:14 put it, started as soon as you became a Christian, and, helped by the Spirit, this life is meant to be one of growth and progress into Jesus' image.

Of course, often we get stuck. We change quite quickly when we first actively follow Jesus, but after a while seem to settle at a certain level of development. Most likely, the people around us can't tell that we've stopped growing but inside we may well feel frustrated or dissatisfied in our faith. Perhaps we are content just to fit in and have an outwardly Christian lifestyle. After all, it's always easier to conform to a culture than it is to truly keep growing. Maybe the people around us aren't pressing further and deeper into their new life in Jesus, so we wonder whether we should. Perhaps we're just not seeking or having the encounters with God that inspired us to follow Jesus in the first place. It was seeing people get stuck in their discipleship for these reasons that motivated me to write this book.

Many people's spiritual life could be likened to the Israelites in the wilderness during the forty years of wandering. You'll remember that they had been released from slavery and called out of Egypt. God had performed miracles of salvation and deliverance to set them free. He had performed miracles of provision and protection on the journey. He had called them into a new relationship, where he had committed himself to be their God and shown them how to walk with him in love. And he had set before them a *"land flowing with milk and honey"* (Exodus 3:8).

Everything was before them... but they couldn't enter. The reports from the men sent into Canaan to spy out the land were full of fear (Numbers 13) and, without faith, it is impossible to enter the Promised Land. What God had set before them was something they couldn't access at that time. It's worth noting that their response, to confess their sins and try harder (Numbers 14:39-40), is simply labelled as "presumption" (verse 44) and the end result is defeat.

You can't get out of the wilderness and into the Promised Land until you've learnt the lessons that God is trying to teach you. For Israel that took a whole generation. What should have been an 11-day journey was to be 40 years (Deuteronomy 1:2). They weren't ready because they refused to trust God's promises. More significantly, they hadn't taken on the new identity that he had given them.

Israel may have got out of Egypt, but there was still a lot of "Egypt" in Israel. Their actions betrayed the fact that they still had a slave identity and a shame mentality. Fear came more naturally than faith. So that to which they were called, the Promised Land, remained closed to them.

Could that be the case in your own discipleship? If you long to walk more closely with Jesus, and share more in what he's doing today, but aren't experiencing any progress, is there something that God has been trying to teach you? If you've been wandering around your own "wilderness", knowing that you're called but repeatedly failing to enter into what he's shown you, then it would definitely be worth setting aside some time to ask him why.

Do you need to come to a fresh realisation of his love for you, that it never needs to be earned and cannot be lost?

Do you truly believe that you are well-pleasing to him, and that he delights in who you are?

Do you know what it is to be his child, and the security and dignity that comes from having such an amazing Heavenly Father?

Do you appreciate the authority that is properly yours as a member of God's royal household?

Do you regularly step forward with that authority so that you're becoming clearer on the ways that God wants to use you uniquely?

Do you experience the joy of fulfilling his plan for your life to the extent that other things lose their appeal?

Where God highlights one of those to you, then that's the place to begin to seek revelation. We receive by faith – which is *"confidence in what we hope for and assurance about what we do not see"* (Hebrews 11:1). He is not withholding anything good from you, so be confident that he is wanting you to make the breakthrough. Simply seek God through prayer, worship and Bible reading, combining what he shows you with faith.

"Without faith it is impossible to please God, because anyone who comes to him must believe he exists and that he rewards those who earnestly seek him." (Hebrews 11:6)

Never question whether God wants to help you grow. He rewards those who earnestly seek him, so determine to be one of those who gets the reward.

Not every breakthrough need be a big or dramatic experience. You don't need to become introspective or self-critical, obsessively checking your own life for evidence of growth. That would be like a gardener constantly uprooting the seeds he'd planted to see whether they had sprouted roots yet! Trust God, take him at his word, and step out in faith.

Stepping out does seem to be an important element in our discipleship. When we read about Jesus with his first disciples, most of the time they seemed slow to grasp the implications of all that he was teaching and showing them. Often he is frustrated with their inability to believe. Yet when the seventy-two return from mission, after he had sent them to preach and heal, they come back changed: *"Lord, even the demons submit to us in your name!"* (Luke 10:17). Jesus' reply is one of exultation – this is what he was longing for all along! Satan was being dethroned (verse 18), God's people were being unleashed and becoming fearless against the enemy (verse 19); they had received revelation (verse 21); and finally the Kingdom of God was coming in power (verse 24). No wonder Jesus is *"full of joy through the Holy Spirit"* (verse 21). His disciples were coming into their true identities – and that is what they should be most excited about (verse 20)!

So think of yourself as a disciple on mission. The way that we learn is by putting God's truth into practice. After all, being like Jesus isn't just a matter of morality but ministry and mission also. He trained his disciples then by sending them, and he trains us today in the same manner.

And remember that Jesus sent them two by two. Don't go alone. The best context for spiritual growth seems to be within a worshiping community on mission. We need each other – and, most likely, you need to learn from people who are further on than you are. Dallas Willard states,

"One thing is for sure: You are somebody's disciple. You learned how to live from somebody else. There are no exceptions to this rule, for human beings are just the kind of creatures that have to learn and keep learning from others how to live. Today, especially in Western cultures, we prefer to think that we are 'our own person'. We make up our own minds. But that is only because we have been mastered by those who have taught us that we do or should do so. Probably you are the disciple of several 'somebodies', and it is very likely that they shaped you in ways that are far from what is best for you, or even coherent. These may include parents, teachers, friends and public figures. It is one of the major transitions of life to recognize who has taught us, mastered us, and then to evaluate the results in us of their teaching. This is a harrowing task, and sometimes we just can't face it. But it can also open the door to choose other masters, possibly better masters, and one Master above all."[3]

Find others who are engaging with this adventure, and share it with them. And, as you learn, pass it on to those who are coming up behind you. Jesus' plan was for discipleship to be a never-ending cascade until all God's people reach their full potential.

One day, we will get there. John says that when Jesus returns, *"We shall be like him, because we shall see him as he is"* (1 John 3:2). Until then, we are daily being changed. As we focus on his glory, we *"are being transformed into his image with ever-increasing glory, which comes from the Lord, who is the Spirit"* (2 Corinthians 3:18). And, whether the path is rough or smooth, he is bending all things into his plan.

"We know that in all things God works for the good of those

who love him, who have been called according to his purpose. For those God foreknew he also pre-destined to be conformed to the image of his Son, that he might be the firstborn among many brothers and sisters" (Romans 8:28-29).

We shall be like him. Enjoy the journey.

Notes

1. Acts 3:8
2. Steven Furtick (@stevenfurtick) on Twitter 13/2/16, from his book, *I Am Unqualified*.
3. Dallas Willard, *The Divine Conspiracy* (Williams Collins, 1998), pp271-272.

About the author

Paul Harcourt leads All Saints' Woodford Wells in NE London, with his wife, Becky, where they have served for 21 years. Paul is New Wine's Regional Director for the London and East Region. Paul is involved in leadership training for renewed churches and regularly speaks at conferences in the UK and Europe. Paul and Becky have two children, Joshua and Rachel, and have learnt a lot about God's grace through coping with Joshua's autism.